THE STORY OF AFRICA

Books One and Two

Ex Africa semper aliquid novi
(Africa always offers something new)

PLINY

THE STORY OF AFRICA

from the earliest times

Book One

A. J. Wills

AFRICANA PUBLISHING CORPORATION
NEW YORK

Published
in the United States of America 1972
by Africana Publishing Corporation
101 Fifth Avenue
New York, N.Y. 10003

Library of Congress Catalog Card No. 72–86247

ISBN 0 8419 0128 7

Printed in Great Britain

Preface

A great deal that is new has been written about African history in the past few years. Much of it has already reached the schools in the form of regional histories. These tell the story of African peoples during the long centuries before the exploration and partition of the nineteenth century. Syllabuses are beginning to cover more of this early period, instead of mainly confining themselves to the past one hundred and fifty years.

However, there still appears to be a need for an overall history of Africa for junior secondary schools which treats the continent and its peoples as a whole and sets their history in the perspective of world developments since ancient and classical times. Such a course can provide the basis of a more detailed regional study later. The political organization of Africa today divides a continent many of whose peoples have a related origin, and none of whom exist in isolation. It would seem reasonable that African children in the different regions should learn about the origin and history of people in other regions. They would also gain a better understanding of how their own background fits into the whole.

The present books are an attempt to meet this need. I am only too well aware that the material does not always lend itself to the interest of children of junior secondary age, and that parts of it describe the movements of people in general terms which may be difficult to teach. On the other hand it is hoped that the language is simple enough for pupils at this stage, and that there are sufficient maps and illustrations to provide work in notebooks. It is also expected that the teacher will have access to regional histories in the school library from which he can obtain more detailed knowledge for story-telling and explanation about the characters and events related only briefly here. At the end of the book there are some questions suggested for the guidance of the teacher.

This first book describes the origin of man in Africa, the development of the Stone Age, the early civilizations, and their influence, especially that of Egypt, on the African interior.

5

The migrations of Negro, Hamitic and Bantu peoples are then recounted, and the book concludes with the medieval history (if such a term may be used in the African context) of East Africa, both inland and on the coast.

The medieval period in West Africa, and later developments throughout the continent, follow in the second book.

A. J. W.

Contents

Acknowledgments

The author and publisher are grateful to the following for permission to reproduce the photographs on the pages indicated:

Aerofilms Ltd: 17 (upper), 42, 86, 104; Barnaby's Picture Library: 63; The Director, British Institute of History and Archaeology in East Africa: 120 (lower); Trustees of the British Museum: 41 (left), 45 (upper), 50, 53, 80, 99 (lower), 100 (left); British Museum (Natural History): 20, 21, 27 (both); Mr Vincent Brown: 45 (lower), 77; Camera Press Ltd: 10, 56 (upper), 93 (both photographs by Robert Shiell); Mr J. Allan Cash: 103; Mary Evans Picture Library: 24, 26, 36 (both), 49, 113; Mr James Kirkman, Fort Jesus National Park, Mombasa, Kenya, 120 (upper); Mansell Collection: 18 (both), 32, 37, 38, 44, 47, 56 (lower), 60 (upper), 99 (upper); Musée de l'Homme, Paris: 29; Musée du Louvre, Paris: 61; Paul Popper Ltd: 14 (left), 17 (lower), 35, 41 (right), 59, 60 (lower), 64, 67, 68 (both), 76, 79, 83, 84, 85, 89, 91, 100 (right), 118; Radio Times Hulton Picture Library: 14 (right), 40, 58; The Science Museum, London: 12; Thames and Hudson Ltd and Brian Fagan: 106 (from *Southern Africa during the Iron Age*); Unesco/Laurenza: 51 (lower); United Press International (U.K.) Ltd: 19; Historical Monuments Commission of Rhodesia: 104 (lower).

The extracts on pages 73, 95, 107–8 and 114 are taken from *The African Past* by Basil Davidson. They are reproduced by permission of Longmans, Green and Co. Ltd.

1 Finding out about history

This book is about the people who have lived in Africa from the very beginning. Africa's history is a very long story. As with any story, it is a good thing to start at the beginning, and this is what we have done.

The early history of man is rather difficult to read about, because we know so little and can only guess what happened from the evidence. Chapter 2 has been written about this early history, or pre-history, partly because scientists today believe that Africa was the home of early man, partly to make the story complete, and partly because some of you might find it interesting. Others may of course prefer to leave it out and go on to Chapter 3.

In more modern times Africa has been populated by many different peoples, and today it is made up of many different nations. Each of you belongs to one of those nations, and in your school or library there will be books telling the story of your own country in more detail. Here we have tried to tell the story of Africa as a whole, so that you can find out something about the other parts besides your own, and see how it all fits together.

The story told in these two books ends in about 1850. The colonial period which comes after that is a separate part of Africa's history which it is best to study on its own. Recently a great deal has been found out about the long history of Africa before the colonial period began, and that is what these books are about.

The reason why it took so long for historians to find out about Africa's past was the absence of written records. Even today much work is being done to find out the true facts in the history of the African peoples. Let us look first at some of the different ways in which this can be done.

How we know about the past

To find out about events which happened a short time ago is not very difficult. Let us suppose that we wanted to find out what happened in Kampala on 20 September, 1960. The first thing we should do would be to go to our national library and look up the newspapers which reported those events. We could study pictures and films which people made at the time. By taking a little more trouble, we could obtain letters written to their friends by eyewitness observers; or we could talk to those observers ourselves. We could examine official reports made by the government, or we could read books that have since been written about the subject.

If, however, we wanted to know what was happening a hundred years earlier, in 1860, it would be more difficult. There were no newspapers in that part of Africa then, and even in Europe the camera had only just been invented. Few, if any, people knew how to write, and official reports were not written by the Buganda government of that time. We could perhaps discover the diary of an educated traveller who had passed through the country, such as James Grant or John Speke, both of whom in fact were in Uganda four years later. An Arab trader might have left some kind of a record in a coastal town. Lastly, there might be an elderly citizen who could remember what his grandparents had told him; but such a report could hardly be an accurate one.

If we think of five hundred years earlier still—thirty generations ago—it becomes impossible for us to know what happened on any particular day, or even in any particular year, over great parts of Africa. Events in West Africa, it is true, during this 'middle age', are better known. This is because the religion of Islam had been spreading there from about 1100. There was more education, and visitors from Arab countries wrote about what they saw. But in most of this huge continent, the life of the people went unrecorded.

Preliterate history

None the less, more is being discovered all the time about this 'preliterate' part of our history—that is, about the time before people knew how to write. Let us look at some of the ways in which this can be done.

First there is the study of language. The growth of a language is part of the growth of a people. Once a language is formed, it continues as long as the people who speak it keep together.

This helps us a great deal. For instance, one people or tribe may split up into groups which wander, taking their languages with them. As time goes by, these languages gradually change as the wandering group mixes with other groups. They become more and more unlike the original language. However, certain 'key' words can still be recognized as having come from the original language. Such a word is *mother* in the European group of languages. Appearing as *mutter, madre, mère* and *mader* in different countries, we can trace it back to *mat,* which is the word for 'mother' in Northern India. We can therefore tell that the people of Europe and the people of northern India long ago had common ancestors. In the same way, many people in different parts of Africa use the word *muntu* for 'man', and *bantu* for 'people'. We can group these people together as having had common ancestors and a common origin. We call them 'Bantu-speaking people'.

Another way in which language can help us is when new words come in from outside. For instance, some African tribes today have Portuguese words in their language, even though they now live far from the Portuguese. Others have Arabic words, even though they now live far from any Arabs. We know therefore that such tribes must have had contact with the Portuguese or with the Arabs at some time in the past.

In the same way, customs can tell us much about the past movements of a tribe or people. There might be a custom about drinking milk from wooden bowls. Or there might be a custom about a son inheriting from his mother instead of from his father. Different tribes which have the same customs, though living in different places, were probably linked together at some earlier time.

A total eclipse of the sun. The moon has come exactly between the sun and the earth

A useful study, of course, is that of folklore or legend. People in Africa, as in other countries, always told their stories from father to son. Sometimes there was one man in the tribe who was given the special task of remembering. Many of these stories are still told. Of course they are not all exactly true. But we can compare them with other knowledge, judge what parts are true, and write them down.

Sometimes science supports folklore. Once a Frenchman sat listening to the elders of a Congo village as they recited the past chiefs of their tribes. The list went on and on. Suddenly the Frenchman leapt to his feet. Something vital had been said. On a certain day in the reign of the ninety-eighth chief, he was told, the world was unexpectedly plunged in darkness for half an hour. The Frenchman went home and studied the astronomical records. He found that an eclipse of the sun had affected that part of the Congo in the year 1680. He was therefore able to give a date to the reign of that chief, and so to other events. In the same way we know the very hour of the day on which the Ngoni forded the Zambezi in 1835.

Archaeology

Even if we do not know the language, or the customs, or the legends of a people who once lived, we can still find out a lot about them. This is because people always leave things behind. Sometimes they drop things by accident. Sometimes they throw things away on purpose because they are of no more use, like a broken pot or a worn tool. Sometimes of course there are tombs or buildings that were purposely made to last. For instance there are the pyramids of the Pharaohs in the north, the houses of ancient Kumbi in the west, and the temple of Zimbabwe in the south, where stone still stands upon stone in spite of the rain and sand and winds of time. The study of these relics of man's past is called *archaeology*.

Many relics disappear for ever. Hot sun, water and insects in the ground cause wood, bone and leather to perish. But stones and stone tools, gold and copper ornaments, glass and pottery remain intact, although they are slowly covered up by the soil. When we find them, perhaps by accident, perhaps by digging on purpose, we are finding clues which can tell us about people who once lived long ago.

Digging up the past

Let us imagine a cave, or a rock shelter. Let us suppose that the first people who lived in this cave were Stone Age hunters,

*Stages in the occupation
of a cave dwelling*

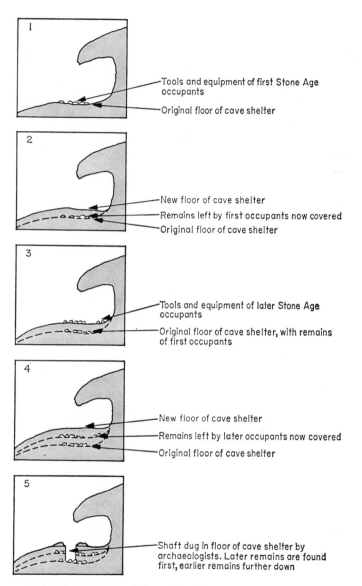

1

Tools and equipment of first Stone Age occupants

Original floor of cave shelter

2

New floor of cave shelter

Remains left by first occupants now covered

Original floor of cave shelter

3

Tools and equipment of later Stone Age occupants

Original floor of cave shelter, with remains of first occupants

4

New floor of cave shelter

Remains left by later occupants now covered

Original floor of cave shelter

5

Shaft dug in floor of cave shelter by archaeologists. Later remains are found first, earlier remains further down

thousands of years ago. They lived here for a long time. During this time, they threw away some of their old possessions, such as worn axes or broken arrowheads. At last they moved from the cave, leaving some more of their things behind.

For a long time after they left, no one lived in the cave. Dust

(Left) Servant's coffin being removed from the remains of an Egyptian palace

(Right) Pit burial dating from the Stone Age in Egypt

and dead leaves blew in. Moss grew, and soil gradually collected. After a few thousand years, several inches of earth covered the floor of the cave once used by the Stone Age hunters.

Now let us suppose that a new set of people came to live in the cave. Perhaps they were early herdsmen, with sheep and goats. They had quite a different set of tools. Some of these became worn out and were thrown away. These later inhabitants lived in the cave for perhaps a thousand years. But the climate was changing. For this, or for some other reason, these new inhabitants also moved away. Again, leaves and dust and soil collected. After a long time, layers of earth covered the old floor.

If we found this cave today, we might guess that men had once lived in it long ago. In order to find out, we would dig a hole in the floor of the cave. We would dig very carefully, sifting through every inch of soil. Soon we would come upon some relics of early herdsmen. Beneath this, we would find a layer with no relics. Deeper still, we would find some relics of Stone Age hunters. We should then be right to suppose that the relics found nearer to the surface belonged to later people. The relics found deeper in the ground must have belonged to earlier people. By measuring the depth of the ground, we could work

Stages in the erosion of a valley (cross section). Stone Age settlements have moved down the hillside, so the earlier settlements are higher up.

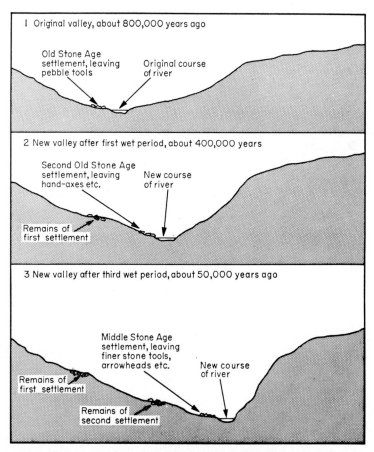

1 Original valley, about 800,000 years ago

Old Stone Age settlement, leaving pebble tools

Original course of river

2 New valley after first wet period, about 400,000 years

Second Old Stone Age settlement, leaving hand-axes etc.

New course of river

Remains of first settlement

3 New valley after third wet period, about 50,000 years ago

Middle Stone Age settlement, leaving finer stone tools, arrowheads etc.

New course of river

Remains of first settlement

Remains of second settlement

out how long ago those people had lived in the cave.

There is one other way of telling how old relics are. Some of these relics may be of wood. Wood contains carbon, but carbon slowly changes its nature with the passage of time. By placing the wood under a special radio wave, scientists can tell how much change has taken place. This kind of measurement is called 'radio-carbon dating'. It can only be used in the case of wood, so it does not help us when the relics are of stone or bone, which contain no carbon.

By using these methods, we are slowly finding out more and more about the prehistory of Africa and other continents. In the next chapter you will read about some of the things scientists have found out about the story of the very earliest men.

2 Stones and future men

Human creatures more or less like ourselves have lived on the continents of the earth for over half a million years.

Half a million years is such a long time that we ought to pause for a moment and think what it means. Consider this book which you are now reading. It contains about 35,000 words made up of about 200,000 letters. That is less than a quarter of a million, but if each letter represents a year, then the number of letters in *three* copies of the book would represent the number of years during which there has been human life. One line in the text would represent the lifetime of one man, two lines a century.

Again, if the height of a telegraph pole were to represent the length of time in which there have been humans, the thickness of a coin placed flat on top of the pole would represent the lifetime of one man.

At the beginning of this time, of course, these early human creatures were in many ways different from modern man. For a million years before that, perhaps longer, they had been developing from a creature that was the ancestor of both apes and men. They were still very like apes in appearance, but they were changing very gradually.

To help us to understand this change, we must try to answer two questions. First, how and why did early man evolve—that is, develop—into a new creature? Second, in what ways did he become different from the early apes?

Evolution

People used to think that men were created simply as men. Many African legends tell how man first came on to the earth and gained mastery over the animals. The story of the Creation in the Hebrew Book of Genesis and in the Koran is well known. These stories are early attempts to explain the creation of man and his relationship with God.

About one hundred and fifty years ago, scientists began to ask themselves how it all happened. How did the Earth begin? How did life start? For years an Englishman, Charles Darwin, made a careful study of plants and animals all over the world. In 1859 he wrote a book called *The Origin of Species* in which he showed that all creatures, whether insects, birds, reptiles or

The long-necked giraffe feeds from the tops of trees

Charles Darwin

mammals had slowly come to their present forms from earlier forms. In struggling to survive against heat and cold, hunger and attack from other creatures, the strongest, best protected and most intelligent had survived. They had produced more of their own kind. Of their offspring, again, some had survived better than others.

So it was that some zebra, for example, survived better because with their striped skins they could be seen less easily in the tall grasses. Some giraffes survived better because with their long necks they were more able to reach the leaves on which they liked to feed. Short-necked giraffes slowly disappeared. Some insects survived because they looked like plants and were hard to see.

So also it was with early apes. Some survived because, with long arms and strong fingers, they could swing more easily from tree to tree. Others did better because they learned to stand upright and run on the ground. This helped them when the climate became dry, and the trees stood farther apart, or there was only grassland. They were able to find roots and new vegetable foods, which made them stronger and more able to protect themselves.

Towards the first men

Now we come to the second question. What were the differences between early apes and early men?

First, they slowly became different in bodily form. Some of these creatures were learning to stand erect and move about in an upright position. Their hands, now used less for clinging to

The hand of the ape and the hand of man evolved differently

the branches of trees, and more for grubbing for roots and collecting vegetables and even animal foods, were changing in form, so that the thumb acted contrary to the fingers. In this way the hands could grasp wood and stone, which could thus be used for special purposes.

Second, in thinking about these purposes and in learning to balance in an upright position, early man gradually developed a larger and more complicated brain.

So it was that a new creature, early man, began to appear among the different kinds of early ape in the warmer regions of Africa. He stood upright more often than on all fours. Instead of five fingers on each hand he had four fingers and a thumb. His skull was larger than that of most apes.

As the centuries gathered into thousands of years, these early men lived more and more differently from the apes. Not only did their bodies become more and more different: their minds developed, so that they began to have the power of language and the ability to reason things out. Moreover, there were various kinds of early man. In the end, all these various kinds disappeared except one. But thousands of years were to pass before this happened.

Changes in climate

We have seen that these creatures slowly changed into new forms because some kinds survived better than others. Why could the others not survive, and just go on living as before? An important reason was that the climate of the world changed from time to time.

Climate is a matter of temperature and rainfall. At some periods in the long distant past the Earth has become a little cooler. When this has happened, the ice that covers the polar regions has spread farther north and south. These times are called 'Ice Ages'. There have been four Ice Ages during the time of early man. The last one was about fifty thousand years ago, when ice covered much of Europe and Asia.

At such a time there was more rain in Africa. Forests were thicker, and parts which are now desert were covered with grass and trees. Even parts of the Sahara were rich grassland.

After a long time of wet climate, the rain would gradually become less, and dry country would begin to return. When this happened, the creatures that flourished in thick forest found it more difficult to live. Early men, however, had better brains and could think how to adjust themselves to changed conditions. Thus they lived most commonly in the grassy country that lay between thick forest and dry desert.

The Early Stone Age begins

Northern Tanzania and Kenya have this kind of grassy country. About half-way between Lake Nyanza and Mount Kilimanjaro, the Rift Valley passes from north to south. Through the floor of the valley, a stream has cut a deep winding gorge. The gorge is about half a mile across, and has steep walls about three hundred feet high.

This is the Olduvai Gorge. One million years ago, when there was more rain in Africa, there used to be a lake here. By the side of the lake lived some creatures who were perhaps some of the earliest men. If we met one of them today, we might think he was a kind of ape. He had a large jaw containing huge teeth, which is why he has been named 'Nutcracker Man'. One reason why he is believed to have been a man is the presence, near the remains of his skull, of some crude stone tools.

Digging for human remains in Olduvai Gorge, Tanzania

Map to illustrate Stone Age sites mentioned in this chapter

- ■ Early Stone Age site
- ▲ Middle Stone Age site
- ● Late Stone Age site

What Australopithecus *may have looked like*

The use of stones as tools was one of the first signs that early man was becoming different from early apes. At first these stone tools were no more than sharp pebbles. After a long time, early men found that they could make certain kinds of pebble sharper by flaking pieces off the side. When this happened, the Stone Age had really begun.

Scientists believe that the Stone Age probably began in South and East Africa. It may even have started at a settlement near the Olduvai Gorge. The first creature to use stone tools has been called *Australopithecus*, a long word which just means 'southern ape'. But remember that he was not really an ape, but an early man. Bones of this creature have been found not only at Olduvai, but also at Sterkfontein and Swartkraans in the Transvaal, and at Taungs in Botswana.

Pithecanthropus and the hand-axe

The Early Stone Age went on for a very long time, perhaps 800,000 years. During this time, however, there were four big changes. These were partly brought about by changes in climate, as the rainfall increased and then decreased again.

First, early men gradually migrated from one continent to another. Probably starting from Africa, they moved to Southern Europe, to Asia and to Indonesia. No remains of these early men have been found in North or South America, so we do not believe they were there.

Second, new kinds of early man began to develop. The name given by scientists to the most important of these new kinds is *Pithecanthropus*, which means 'Ape Man'. He was a more advanced kind of early man. He had a straighter back, longer legs and a larger skull—though this was still only three-quarters the size of modern man's. He was five feet tall and had a thick neck and a heavy ridge over his eye; his teeth were still very much longer than ours.

The best remains of these new early men have been found not in Africa but in the Far East of Asia. One discovery was in Java, part of what is now Indonesia. The most important discovery was in a cave near Peking in China.

Hand-axe

However, there have been finds in Africa as well. Dr Louis Leakey, the scientist who made the discovery, gave the name *Zinjanthropus* to this kind of early man. Another find was made in 1955 in a sandpit near Ternifine in Algeria. Here the bones of early men very like Peking Man were found, together with the bones of animals such as the sabre-toothed tiger, and several stone tools.

This brings us to the third important change. During this long period of time, man had learnt to make wonderful stone tools. Stone tool-making had become a craft. The commonest of these tools was the hand-axe. This was what we should now call an axe-head. It was carefully chipped from a large flint, and held in the hand for cutting. It was also used for chopping at wood, bone, sinew and meat. A big hand-axe could measure nine inches long, but most were five or six inches in length.

Another stone tool was flatter in shape. This was the cleaver. It was used for scraping flesh and fat from the inside of skins, which man would use for covering himself. It was also used for splitting wood.

The use of fire

The fourth important change was one of the greatest discoveries in the history of man. By the end of the Early Stone Age, he had learnt to make and use fire.

Fire was not new to man. Fires started naturally from time to time. Volcanoes erupted, and their sparks set light to the forest. Lightning during a storm could also set fire to trees. These fires were strange and to be feared. Early man had always kept away from fire.

When flaking stone tools, however, men saw the sparks fly. By accident—many great discoveries are made by accident—some sparks fell one day on dry grass, and a fire was started. Soon men learnt not only how to make fire, but also how to control it.

Fire was soon found to be useful in many ways. It provided warmth at night and in the cold season. Meat cooked in fire was better to eat and lasted longer than raw meat. Fire gave protection, because wild animals were afraid of it. A fire burning in the mouth of a cave allowed a family to sleep safely at night. Early men began to settle in caves or rock shelters instead of moving about all the time. Fire also helped in hunting, as we shall see in the next chapter.

We know that early men like *Pithecanthropus* used fire, because layers of ash have been found with the stone tools in the places where he lived. One of these places is near the Kalambo Falls in Northern Zambia.

The Sangoans of the Middle Stone Age

By about 50,000 years ago, early men were much more like men today. They always walked upright, and their brains were bigger than those of any ape. They made many different kinds of tool, and their hand-axes and cleavers were smaller and sharper.

The bones of this kind of man have been found at Neanderthal in Switzerland. He is known as Neanderthal Man. The skull of another but similar kind of man was dug out of Broken

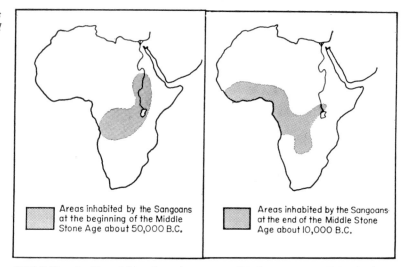

Areas inhabited by the Sangoans at the beginning of the Middle Stone Age about 50,000 B.C.

Areas inhabited by the Sangoans at the end of the Middle Stone Age about 10,000 B.C.

Hill Mine in Zambia a few years ago. He is known as Rhodesian Man.

Over most of Africa, however, there lived in this Middle Stone Age a type of early man whom we call Sangoan. The name comes from Sango Bay on the western shore of Lake Nyanza, where remains of this type were first found. The Sangoans lived in greater numbers than their predecessors. They made fire, lived in rock shelters, they could carry burdens on their backs, and they had better tools. The Sangoans peopled all tropical Africa between the Sahara in the north and the Zambezi in the south.

South of the Zambezi lived a similar people, whose culture is called Fauresmith after the South African township where their remains were first discovered.

Homo sapiens

But the Sangoans, like other Middle Stone Age men, also disappeared in the end, to be replaced by Modern Man, or *Homo sapiens*. The reason for their disappearance was the coming of one more great change of climate.

This was the last Ice Age, which covered Europe and Asia with ice and snow for thirty thousand years. Heavy rain and thick forest again spread over Africa. When this rainy period ended about ten thousand years ago, the only human creatures left were the type which we know today, and which is called *Homo sapiens* or 'Thinking Man'.

23

3 Hunters and artists

In our story of early men, we have reached the time of about 10,000 years ago. We have seen how the very earliest men probably developed in Africa itself. From there they wandered slowly from Africa to Europe and Asia. Some of them made their way back to Africa. As the climate changed, men looked for better homelands and changed their way of life.

Ten thousand years ago, the last time of very wet climate was passing away. The Sahara was still rich grassland, with swamps full of game, but it was slowly becoming dry. The thick forests of Africa were becoming smaller. Except for the West African rain forest and the Congo basin, these forests were being replaced by open country with trees and grassland.

Early kinds of man had disappeared. Only modern man, thinking man, whom we call *Homo sapiens*, was left.

Late Stone Age Man in Africa

Although man was of the same kind, he was in different families. These different families are often called races.

In Africa at this time there were four different families of men. First were the ancestors of the Bushmen of today. They were small, of light build and with light brown skins. They lived in the highlands of East, Central and Southern Africa, where they were great hunters.

Hunting for hippopotamus

Second were the Pygmies and Negrilloes. They were probably related to the Bushmen. They preferred to stay in the thick rain forests of the northern Congo basin. They were slightly darker in colour than the Bushmen and remained very small in size. Some people think they used to be larger, but became smaller owing to the difficulty of life in the thick forest.

The third family was that of the Negroes. They lived in the Sudan, all the way from the Upper Nile and its tributary, the Bahr-el-Gazal, to the Niger. They hunted in the grasslands of the Sahara and the swamps of Lake Chad. They had formerly lived in the forests, and as the climate became drier they still preferred to live along the river banks and lake sides where they could fish and find river game. Later, as we shall see, they became some of the first settled farmers. They were taller than the Bushmen and had very dark brown skins. We do not know where they came from, but their origin is discussed in Chapter 9.

Fourth was a family of people who had come into Africa from Palestine, about nine thousand years ago. They were an early kind of Hamite, and were dark brown in colour. Some went to North Africa, and hunted in the northern Sahara. Remains of these people have been found at Gafsa in Tunisia. They are therefore sometimes called Capsian people. Others like them went to East Africa and settled down in the Rift Valley. Here they made very fine stone tools with long, thin blades.

Later in this book you will read more about Hamites, or Hamitic people. They are supposed to be descended from Ham, who was the second son of Noah, the great Hebrew leader described in the Book of Genesis and the Koran.

Hunting

All these families of late Stone Age people were great hunters. They did not yet know how to grow crops or how to keep animals. They still lived by gathering roots from the ground; and fruits and berries from trees, and by hunting wild game. Early Stone Age men had lived like this for thousands of years, but by this time better ways had been invented of doing these things. Because of this men had more food to eat, and so they slowly increased in numbers.

For example, fire was now used for hunting. By lighting a grass fire when the wind was in the right direction, men could drive animals into a lake or swamp where they could be killed in great numbers.

*Hunting elephant
with a pit trap*

Secondly, men used now to dig pit traps. These would be dug along trails used by animals going to water. The pit would be concealed with grass and leaves, and at the bottom sharpened

Bone piercing tool from the Late Stone Age

wooden stakes would be planted. The points of the stakes had been hardened in fire.

Of course, men still hunted with spears, but these spears were better than before. The stone points were much sharper. In East Africa, the barb was invented. This was a hook near the end of the spear, to prevent it from falling out when it pierced flesh. It was made of a small curved flake of stone. Before long, man learnt to make a barbed spear point out of bone. This was not strong enough to kill a large animal, but was useful for catching fish in the lakes of East Africa and in the Nile.

Another throwing weapon was a stone placed on the end of a wooden handle. The stone had a hole bored through the centre, into which the handle was driven. Men learnt to throw this a long way with accuracy.

The bow for shooting arrows was one of the most important weapons invented in the Late Stone Age. The bowstring was made of sinew. Arrow-heads were made from small flakes of stone. Many different kinds of arrow-head have been found in Africa, dating from these times.

Men also learnt to conceal themselves while hunting, by decorating their bodies with coloured pigments taken from the earth. These colours were mostly white, red and yellow, but grey, blue and green were also used. Men also found that to decorate themselves in this way was an exciting thing to do. It made them feel important.

Other inventions

Once men had started to invent things, there was no end to it. Right down to the present day, man has been inventing ways of obtaining more food, and of making life safer and more comfortable. Sometimes, of course, he has made life more dangerous for himself. Most inventions have good and bad uses. The first invention was the stone tool. One of the most recent has been nuclear power.

Two very important inventions were made in the Late Stone Age in Africa. The first was the needle. This was made out of bone. A long, thin, pointed bone with a hole at one end could be used to draw string, made of sinew, through skins to join them together. Stone Age man had learnt to work as a tailor. He could make simple clothes, which could keep him warm in the cold season. Clothes were not always made of skins. Man learnt also to make fabric from leaves and from the bark of

Barbed arrow-head (about 2½ in. long)

27

trees. He used gums and resins to improve these fabrics. Skins were used more often in the northern countries of Europe and Asia, where the weather was much colder in the winter, as compared with tropical Africa.

The second invention made by Stone Age man in Africa was the clay pot. This most important discovery was made by the early Hamitic people of the Rift Valley in Kenya. Pots were useful for storing food and water. They were also useful for cooking. They made a great difference in the home life of Stone Age man.

The first pots were made from baskets lined with clay. Then it was found that if the pot was placed on the fire, the grass of the basket burnt away and the baked clay became hard and strong. After this, pots were made out of clay without the basket. But to remind people of the marks of the basket these new pots were decorated with lines.

Different peoples decorated their pots in different ways. Thus, when a piece of pottery is found that was made long ago, we can usually tell, by looking at the decoration, who it was that made it.

A third invention of the Late Stone Age was the small stone tool. Until now, stone tools had been fairly big, with pieces chipped off the edge. Now some of the chips were made into tiny stone tools. This is how arrow-heads and the barbs on spears were made. The Capsian people of Tunisia and of Kenya made fine long-bladed tools. With these tools, they carved wood and bone. The Nachikufu people of Zambia also made fine little stone tools. Yet another kind of small stone tool was made by the Wilton people of Rhodesia and South-West Africa. The Smithfield people of South Africa also made stone tools of this kind.

All these Late Stone Age peoples have been named after present-day places where their tools have recently been found. Some photographs are shown on page 27. The Wilton tools were probably the finest of all.

Rock art

The inventions that have just been described were made between about 10,000 and 5,000 years ago. During that time, Late Stone Age man made another great discovery, quite different from the others. This was the art of painting pictures.

This discovery was different, because the others were all

directly useful to man. The painting of pictures was not useful in the same way. It was important because it expressed the thoughts of man. It was the first step in the long road to the invention of writing. Men could begin to gather knowledge. They could give their thoughts, not only to their fellow men, but also to the generations of men who came afterwards.

We have seen how men had already learnt to decorate their bodies with coloured earth. This helped them in hunting. After a time it was also used for dances and magical rites. Now they began to paint designs on the rock walls of the caves and shelters where they lived.

Many of these paintings are found in the Tassili and Tibesti hills of the central Sahara. On smooth walls of the rocky hill-sides you can see pictures of giraffe and elephant and hippo-potamus. There are beautiful drawings of cattle. There are also pictures of men hunting, and herding cattle, and of women at work. These pictures show how the Sahara was once rich grass-land with lakes and rivers and much wild game. They also show how clever an artist Stone Age man had become four or five thousand years ago.

Other rock paintings are in Southern Africa. Some can be seen in Rhodesia; others in the Orange Free State. These too show hunting scenes in which men chase many different kinds of wild animal. The animals are beautiful and strong. The men are brave and run fast. They shoot their arrows and throw their spears.

Stone Age rock drawing
of a hunter
and his dog,
from Tassili, Sahara.
The hunter
has a dog's head

*Bushman pattern design
from the Transvaal*

These are some of the finest paintings in the world. Artists today admire them. They have lasted in the open air for thousands of years.

Few of these pictures show men fighting against one another. In those days, men hunted animals but did not fight amongst themselves. There was no need: men were few and there was enough land for all to hunt in, provided they were brave.

Why did men start to paint these pictures? We do not know for certain. Probably they believed it helped them in their hunting. They admired the animals: they wanted to be strong like the elephant and run fast like the antelope. Perhaps also they were sorry for the animal when it was killed. The picture seemed to make it come alive again. They were reminded, besides, of a great hunt and of the hunters. They were beginning to record the story of man.

Finally, it is possible they thought there was magic in the picture. Some of the later paintings are strange shapes that we do not understand. The people of Nachikufu made some of the 'pattern' designs. Others were done by the rock painters of the Sahara.

Religious belief

These pictures seem to tell us that Late Stone Age man was beginning to fear and to worship spirits. He did not understand these spirits. Perhaps he thought they were in the thunder and the lightning; or in the animals he hunted; or in people who had died.

One more 'invention' of Late Stone Age man tells us that this was so. He began to bury people with care. He did not yet make tombs as men later learnt to do. But sometimes a dead man was buried deep in the ground, sitting up, surrounded with the pots and weapons he had used in life. This was done by the Late Stone Age people of Kenya.

When man buried people like this, it shows that he was beginning to believe in a life after death.

Man at the end of the Late Stone Age

Thus, by about 5000 B.C., man had made great progress. True, he still only lived in families or groups of families, and did not have a proper chief. He did not know how to grow food, nor did he know how to keep tame animals—except perhaps the dog, the oldest friend of man.

However, man knew how to make many kinds of equipment to help him in his life. He knew how to express himself in painting and perhaps—though we shall never know—in music. He believed in spirits that were outside himself and stronger than himself. He was man the worker, man the artist, and man the worshipper. He had become a full man.

Man was ready for the great step forward which we shall read about in the next chapter.

4 Farmers of the Nile

The use of fire, as we have seen, encouraged men to live in caves. However, men were still hunters and collectors of food. Groups could not settle down and stay in one place for any length of time until they had learnt to *produce* food.

The first farmers

The first people who found out how to plant seed in the ground in order to grow their own food lived in Asia.

About ten thousand years ago, some Stone Age people on the southern shores of the Caspian Sea began to grow and reap grain crops. They must often have noticed how the seeds of wheat and barley plants, which grew wild, would fall on the ground and grow into new plants the next season. It was already known that wheat grains and barley grains were good to eat. Now someone thought of collecting some seeds and planting them all in one place. The experiment was successful. It was a great discovery, because it was the beginning of agriculture.

Other inventions began to follow—simple wooden hoes to scratch the soil, bone sickles to cut the crop, baskets to hold the grain, pestles and mortars to grind it.

At about the same time these people began to keep their own sheep and goats. These animals provided them with meat

Egyptian tomb painting showing early Nile farmers using hoes and sowing seeds

*Where agriculture started
in the Middle East
about 6,000 years ago*

and milk. They no longer had to go out and hunt for their food supply.

Few people lived like this, by farming. Most people went on wandering about, collecting food. Men were few in those days, and they were outnumbered by animals of all kinds. However, the first farmers were able to live better and have more food than other people. Slowly, in one or two places, other people began to copy them. For instance, there were some early farmers at Jericho in Palestine about this time. There was a spring there which never dried up, so that there was always water as well as sunshine. This meant that there was good ground where plants could grow.

The Nile

About eight thousand years ago, a group of wandering people from Palestine crossed the country of Sinai. Sinai is between Asia and Africa. For thousands of years people had wandered across it from Africa to Asia, and from Asia to Africa, in this

33

way. Today it is desert, but it was then rolling grassland. These people came to a river valley of forest and swamp, and through the forest flowed a great river. That river was the Nile.

It was the biggest river they had ever seen. The forest and swamps were too thick for farming, but among the low hills to the west there was a lake, from which streams flowed down to the river. This place is today called the Fayyum oasis. Beside the lake they cleared a place for their village of simple huts, and sowed some seeds. The ground was good, and crops grew well. As the years passed, other people came to live there, and a settlement of farmers was begun.

Many generations passed: one hundred years, then five hundred years, then a thousand years. All the time the climate was becoming drier and drier. It rained less and less as the centuries went by. The lake grew smaller, and people had to move their villages to keep near the shore. The grassland began to become a desert, and it was harder to grow crops.

Down in the valley by the great Nile River, the forest became thin and the swamp began to dry. After another very long time there were fewer trees, and most of them grew along the banks of the river. About this time, the farming people left the dry ground by the hills and came to live on the flat floor of the valley itself. To make space they even cut down some of the trees that were left.

The floods

The farming people had long known a very important fact about the Nile. Every year in the late spring, much more water, black with mud, used to flow down the river and overflow the banks. These floods came, in fact, because every year heavy rains fell in the mountains of far-off Ethiopia. The early farmers of the Nile did not know this: they only saw how the river would burst its banks and flood wide parts of the valley. Then, after some months, the water would sink back and the river would once again be flowing quietly under the hot sun. But, where the floods had been, there was left a rich layer of black mud. This made wonderful earth for growing good crops.

At first, all the farmer had to do was to scatter seed on the rich, moist earth. The seed he used was wheat and barley. This seed would quickly take root and grow into a fine crop, without any digging. The farmer harvested it four months later. He cut it with a sickle, which was made of pieces of flint chipped into

The Lower Nile. The fields reach the water's edge

The life of the Nile valley dwellers

sharp teeth and set into a wooden handle. As more food was produced, the population of the valley began to grow.

When more people lived in the valley, farmers had to use ground which was farther from the river. The ground was not so moist here, so it was necessary to dig a hole for the seed. In order to dig, the farmer used a wooden stick. Sometimes he had a small hoe with a sharpened stone blade which was tied to the wooden handle with a leather thong.

The farmers kept their permanent villages near the flood lands, and lived there during the summer. In the winter months, after the crop had been harvested, they went away to the higher ground and built grass shelters. Here they spent every day hunting, just as people used to do before they learnt to become farmers. Besides lions and leopards, there were elephants and kudu and two kinds of wild pig. Then, after the new flood season, they would return to the valley. These people were therefore still partly hunters and partly farmers.

35

While tne hunters were away on their expeditions, other people with special skills stayed at home. Some of them worked at making stone tools and weapons, because the old ones were always getting broken or blunt. Others made baskets, or carved wood. Others again made pots with clay. Pots were useful for keeping seed, grain and water; also people were learning to cook with their pots. In the river they caught fish, and sometimes hunted crocodile and hippopotamus.

Irrigation

Land was now worked even farther from the river. Here, because there was no rain, the ground was too dry for crops to grow at all. It was necessary to bring water from the river in pots and pour it on the ground.

One day a sensible farmer found that it was easier to make a ditch leading away from the river. If water was poured into the ditch, it ran along to the field where the grain was planted. All that had to be done was to stand by the river bank and lift water in clay-lined baskets, which were bigger than pots, into the ditch. This was hard work, but not as hard as carrying the water all the way to the field.

After a time the *shaduf* was invented for lifting the water out of the river. You can see one of these in the picture. As a result, more and more fields were irrigated, and more and more crops were grown. Later, the water wheel was invented for irrigation. It was called a *tabut* and was worked by an ox.

A shaduf

A tabut

5 Egypt: Towns and temples of stone

The early Hamitic farmers in the Nile valley were able to grow more food than the Negro hunters and herdsmen, because of the Nile flood, and the rich soil it brought from the rainstorms in the mountains of Ethiopia far away.

Towns

Because of this, the population grew. As time went by—a hundred years, five hundred years, again a thousand years— there were more and more people living in the Nile valley. Some of them lived in the delta, where the river splits into branches that run through rich, flat country to the sea. Others lived two hundred miles to the south, where the rock walls of the valley are closer together. Here the valley floor is narrower and the soil is very rich.

At first, people cut down the trees in the valley and built wooden houses. They filled the gaps in the walls with mud and made flat roofs of reeds laid across rafters, covered with clay. At first these people lived in small villages, but slowly the villages grew larger, until one or two of them were really small towns. In the towns, many people did many different kinds of work. There were soldiers to keep order, builders, carpenters, basket-makers, potters and boat-builders. What a difference this was from the simple Stone Age life two thousand years before!

The Nile and the gods

All life centred round the Nile and its floods. Where the waters came from, no one knew, because it hardly ever rained in Egypt. The flood was a gift from the gods. The people began to worship the god who gave the floods and the life of the crops.

Egyptians harvesting, 2000 B.C. (from a wall painting)

The most important god was Re, the sun god, who gave light and warmth and never failed, dying each night but coming to life again each morning. Another god was Osiris who, it was

MEDITERRANEAN SEA

LOWER EGYPT

Giza △
Memphis ●

Fayyum

MIDDLE EGYPT

Mt. Sinai ▲

R. Nile

UPPER EGYPT

Valley of the Kings

● Karnak
● Thebes
● Luxor

Edfu ●

1st Cataract

RED SEA

Abu Simbel ●

0   100   200
Miles

2nd Cataract

NUBIA

Papyrus raft on the Nile

believed, was killed by his wicked brother Seth, his body being cut into pieces and thrown into the Nile. Next spring, Isis, who was wife or perhaps sister of Osiris, found the pieces and brought him to life again. This story meant that Osiris was god of the crops, which came to life when seeds were sown, and Isis was goddess of the river which brought them water.

After a long time the people in the valley became so many that they had to make laws about who should have the land, and how water should be brought to the fields when the floods were small. Groups of villages sometimes fought about the land. After a time of struggles, the people in the narrow part of the Nile valley joined together and formed a single nation. They had a king to lead them. He was believed to be inhabited by the spirit of God, and wore a tall white crown. The nation here called their kingdom Upper Egypt.

Down the river in the delta, also, the tribes joined together to form a kingdom. These people called their kingdom Lower Egypt. Their king was also 'divine', and wore a headdress like a crown, coloured red.

Most of the time there was peace in the Nile valley. Boats were built, and sailed up and down the river between the two kingdoms. Long ago the people had learnt how to make rafts out of bundles of papyrus reeds, which are soft reeds growing in the delta, and which become very light when dry. Later, they discovered that a raft shaped like a boat, hollow in the middle and rising up to a point at both ends, could carry greater loads. At last they found that stronger boats could be made out of wood. Upper Egypt produced more marsh reeds which were used for building. Villagers there exchanged these for papyrus reeds, which mostly grew in the delta.

Sometimes the two kingdoms grew jealous of each other, and fought wars. In the end, a great king of Upper Egypt, called Menes Narmer, was strong enough to join the two kingdoms into one. He styled himself Pharaoh, 'the Royal House', and was known as the Ruler of the Two Lands. He founded a ruling family, which we call a dynasty. This first dynasty started about five thousand years ago.

Five thousand years ago is about 3000 B.C. We count our years from the birth of Christ, and it is easy for us to say that King Mutesa of Buganda lived in A.D. 1880, or that King Menes of the Two Lands lived in 3000 B.C. The Egyptians, of course, could not do this, and when something happened they said it was in a certain year of a certain dynasty, or ruling family. Altogether there were thirty dynasties in Egypt, right up to the time of the Roman Empire.

Menes built a new capital at Memphis, on the border

between Lower Egypt and Upper Egypt on the west bank of the Nile. It became a big town.

By this time trees were becoming scarce in the Nile valley. Houses were built of sun-dried mud bricks instead of wood. Mud bricks lasted a long time, because there was so little rain. The king's palace was also built of bricks, but the temples where the priests worshipped the sun god were built of stone. The temples were supposed to last for ever. The stone was quarried from the cliffs overlooking the valley floor.

Trade

The soil in the valley and the delta was so good that an Egyptian landowner was able to grow two or three times as much food as he needed to feed his family and the families of his farm workers. He was able to sell the extra to people who did other work and who did not grow food. He could then buy the things which they made in exchange.

The rich man was able to buy wooden doors and windows for his house, and cloth from flax spinners and weavers, for making clothes and shady awnings. He could buy implements for his workers and pots for cooking, and jewellery for his wife and daughters. On special occasions he could buy wine and expensive foods.

Some of the extra food produced could be sold in the market of a nearby town. A trader would send it to another part of Egypt. More and more boats sailed up and down the Nile. Those which went down the river needed no sail. Those which went up the river had to have a sail to move them against the current. Occasionally a boat even sailed out into the Mediter-

One of the ships on the expedition to Punt (from a wall painting)

ranean Sea, though Egyptian sailors were afraid of the sea. About 2500 B.C. a Pharaoh had a canal dug from the delta to the Red Sea. Sometimes Egyptian boats went into the Red Sea. About 1480 B.C., Queen Hatshepsut sent an expedition along the Red Sea as far as the land of Punt on the east shore of the Red Sea and it came back with a cargo of ivory, tortoise-shell and cypress wood.

Another part of the produce of the rich farmer had to be paid to the king in taxes. The king became very rich, and was able to buy gold and ornaments of a blue stone called *lapis lazulae*, and to have great statues made and palaces built.

Tombs

Most Egyptian kings spent a great deal of time preparing wonderful tombs in which their bodies would be preserved after they were dead. They believed that their life-soul or *Ka* would live after death, and would need the body. Therefore the body had to be preserved.

This was done, after death, by filling the body with special

(Below) Mummy cover of a priestess lying in her coffin (about 1300 B.C.)

(Right) Djoser's step pyramid

ointments and resins, and wrapping it in many layers of cloth. This wrapped body, which was called a *mummy*, was placed in a curved box in the shape of a body, with the face of the king painted on the outside. The box was laid in a square coffin. The box and the coffin were decorated with brightly coloured pictures telling about the life of the dead king, and with prayers for his safe journey to the other world. The coffin was placed in an oblong tomb called a *mastaba*, which was often situated at the top of a hill to the west of the Nile. Then people could look towards it in the golden light of sunset. They would think of the king dying with the sun, believing that he would be born again next day.

At first, only the king used to have his body preserved, perhaps because it was so expensive; but later ordinary people also came to believe that their *Ka* would live after death, and had their bodies preserved if they could afford it. But for the mass of the poor people it was never possible.

The Pyramids

The tomb was also furnished with all kinds of useful things to help the king in his next life. There were pots and weapons and ornaments. Although the tombs were guarded, robbers often broke in later to steal valuable things. In order to prevent this, larger and larger tombs were built. King Djoser, about two hundred years after Menes, built a very big tomb, square at the base, with a series of smaller layers on top, rising in steps to a point. This was the first pyramid. It was thirty feet high.

Each of the Pharaohs who came after Djoser wanted to be remembered by even bigger, stronger tombs, and so the Great Pyramids came to be built. They are still to be seen today, at Giza, near the beginning of the delta in Lower Egypt.

Khufu's pyramid, the biggest, was so big that it needed nearly two and a half million blocks of stone. Each block of stone weighed over two tons. Some weighed fifteen tons. There was no suitable stone nearby, so the blocks had to be quarried miles up the river, floated down on rafts, and then dragged over the sand on sledges. The sledges were placed on rollers to help them move along. About 100,000 men, many of them slaves, worked at the building. Others worked in the flood season, after the crops had been collected. It took twenty years for the Great Pyramid to be completed.

The people did not like the hard work very much, but they

The Great Pyramids. The middle one is that of Khufu

thought it was worth while. They were working for the life of the Divine King in the next world, where he would join Re, the sun god, who blessed the land of Egypt.

Early scientific knowledge in Egypt

All these labours in farming, building and religious worship enabled the Egyptians to lay the foundations of a simple scientific knowledge.

Very early in the history of Egypt, the regular coming of the Nile floods was seen to agree with the appearance of certain stars in the sky. The Egyptians studied the stars, and were able to make a simple calendar. By this calendar they planned the planting of crops and the reaping of harvests, and the religious ceremonies that went with them. They also used the shadow made by the sun to tell the time of day. Thus they invented the first clock, and used it to mark the hours of labour.

The building of pyramids and temples called for accurate measurement. The rise and fall of the Nile waters had also to be carefully recorded. Egyptian mathematicians learnt how to make exact levels, and how to construct right-angles. They studied the problems of triangles. Though their knowledge of geometry was simple compared with that of the Greeks later on, the accuracy with which the huge pyramids were built could not be improved upon by engineers today.

In preserving their dead, the Egyptians also learnt a good deal about the human body. They did not understand the importance of the brain, and thought that the heart was the centre of the intelligence. But physicians learnt how to do simple operations, and how to use a number of medicines both from plants such as acacia, anise and castor beans, and from minerals such as arsenic, nitre and sulphur.

In the early days, most of this knowledge was held by the caste of priests, who caused it to be written down on scrolls of papyrus. Many of these scrolls have survived, to be discovered in recent years.

Writing

Indeed, we know all this, and much more, about the Egyptians in the Nile valley because they left so many records of their doings.

We have read in an earlier chapter that Late Stone Age man, in parts of Africa, had already started to paint pictures. The

*Egyptian
picture writing*

people of the Nile learnt—perhaps from these Stone Age Africans, perhaps from the people of Mesopotamia—how to paint pictures also.

However, the Egyptians went further. They invented a system of picture writing. They made a special set of pictures and each represented a word or a sound. The meaning of these picture-symbols was known only to the priests of Amon-Re, who alone were allowed to do the writing. For this reason we call early Egyptian writing *hieroglyphic* from a Greek word *hieros* meaning 'priest'.

This writing is found painted on the coffins of buried people, and carved on temple walls. The stories tell of the lives of Pharaohs, and of great events in the Old Kingdom; and of the legends of the past. This is how we know the story of Isis and Osiris, and other stories about Egyptian gods.

It also became possible to send letters giving instructions to governors in different parts of the kingdom. We have one complete letter that was written at this time. It was sent by the Pharaoh Mernere to Harkhuf, one of his generals.

Harkhuf and the Pygmy

Harkhuf had been sent with an expedition of soldiers and carriers to travel far up the Nile and to find what country lay beyond.

After many weeks, Harkhuf returned. On reaching the border of Upper Egypt, he sent word to the king that he brought ebony, ivory and frankincense from beyond the desert. He also brought a 'dwarf', who must in fact have been a Pygmy.

The king's letter in reply said that Harkhuf must come north to the court at once, and bring the Pygmy. Every care must be taken to see that he came to no harm. 'When he boards the ship (to sail down the Nile), appoint good men to be on each side of him in case he falls into the water.' He had to be guarded at night. 'My majesty desires to see this dwarf more than the gifts of Sinai and Punt.'

We shall never know what happened to the Pygmy. He probably spent the rest of his life at the court of Pharaoh in Memphis, admired by the tall people of the Nile, far from his home in the distant forests of the Congo.

Demotic script

The story of Harkhuf and the Pygmy is copied in hieroglyphic script on the walls of King Mernere's tomb.

Writing in hieroglyphic was difficult and slow. Later the

Egyptians invented a new kind of writing, which we call *demotic script*. This means 'the writing of ordinary people'. It is called this because scribes who were not priests were now taught to write. The signs were no longer pictures, but more simple, like ordinary letters. But there were still many signs, and the Egyptians never invented an alphabet.

The scribe wrote on a kind of paper made from the soft papyrus reed. Indeed, the English word *paper* comes from the name of this reed. The scribe wrote with a split reed which he dipped in water mixed with a finely ground powder made from soot if he wanted black, or from earth if he wanted red.

Until only one hundred and fifty years ago, we could not understand Egyptian writing. Then a stone was found at Rosetta in the Nile delta, on which the same subject was written in hieroglyphic, then in demotic script, and lastly in ancient Greek. We can understand Greek writing. Therefore it was possible for scholars to discover the meaning of the Egyptian picture-symbols and signs. After that, much more of the early history of Egypt became known.

45

6 The age of metals

For a long time the Egyptians, in spite of the civilization they were beginning to create, had remained a Stone Age people.

Most of their tools, weapons and implements continued to be made of stone. The poorest peasants did not even have stone, but dug in the ground with wooden hoes. Richer people, however, had finely made stone ornaments and tools. Stone work had become a great art. Knife blades of flint were thin, polished and quite sharp. People even shaved with them. The royal army was equipped with stone-pointed weapons. Arrow-heads for hunting, harpoon-heads for fishing and spear-heads for fighting were made of hard, sharp flint.

But the Egyptians' greatest achievements were made after they had discovered the use of metals.

Gold

When people were looking about for good pieces of stone for shaping into tools, they sometimes came across pure veins of metal in the rock. They could see that the metal was different from stone.

The metals which the early Nile people found appearing like this in their pure state were gold and silver. They were found in small amounts, so they were very valuable. Gold mostly came from the hill country of Nubia, and here the Egyptians had their gold mines.

Gold was too soft to use as a tool or a weapon, but the Egyptians loved to make it into beautiful things. It never rusts or tarnishes, but lasts seemingly for ever. The Egyptians therefore used gold to decorate the tombs of their kings. They beat it into thin sheets, and moulded these sheets round models made of wood. They used it for ladies' jewels and for rings and bracelets. The handle of the king's dagger was made of gold.

Copper

Copper, a more useful metal, was found quite by accident. Some travellers in Sinai made a fire to warm themselves at night. Heavy greenish stones were used to make the hearth. Later, when the fire cooled, it was seen that a reddish metal had trickled from the hot stones. This was copper, and the stones were copper ore.

*Copper figure of a bison
from Sumeria
(about 2,500 B.C.)*

The Egyptians found that copper was much harder than gold. Yet it would bend without breaking, unlike stone. It could be beaten into shapes, and would make a sharper edge or point than a stone tool or weapon. Copper blades lasted better than stone blades, which were always getting blunt. When a copper tool was finished with, it could be melted down and used for something else.

In Egypt, rich people had copper tools from quite early times, even in the time of the first Pharaoh. The cutting tools that carved the blocks of stone that were used to build the pyramids were made of copper.

None the less, copper ore was rare in the Nile valley. The Egyptians used to import copper from Sinai, and sometimes from Mesopotamia. There, in the valley of the Euphrates, lived the Sumerian people. They used copper even more than the Egyptians. From the people of Mesopotamia, the Egyptians were now to discover an even more useful metal—bronze.

Bronze	The Sumerians built up a fine civilization, but about 1800 B.C. they were conquered by the Semitic people of Babylon. Babylon was a strong kingdom farther up the Euphrates River. Its greatest ruler was Hammurabi, who is famed even now for the laws he made.

The Babylonians were great metal workers, and they now made an important discovery. By this time, other metals were known besides copper, and one of these was tin. The Babylonians found that by mixing a little tin with copper (about 2 oz. to 1 lb.) a new metal alloy was formed, which we call 'bronze'.

Bronze melts more easily than pure copper, and so it was easier to mould into shapes. But once it had set, bronze was harder than copper, and so made better tools. It was also useful for making into weapons. Swords and spearheads, and even shields and helmets for rich people, could be made of bronze. The use of bronze spread quickly through the Middle East.

The wheel	At about the same time, but farther north in Asia, the great invention of the wheel was made.

Ever since trade began long ago, the transport of heavy goods had presented a problem. Where there was a river, goods could be carried by boats. On land, pack animals like mules or donkeys or oxen could be used. Very heavy things such as stone blocks for buildings were dragged along the ground, using wooden logs as rollers to help them move. But even in Egypt, where such rollers were often used, no one thought of the wheel.

On the plains of southern Asia, however, men had learnt to tame and ride horses. Horses were used to pull sledges. Sometimes rollers were placed beneath the sledge. Then the axle was invented so that the roller could be fixed to the sledge. Thus the roller became the wheel. The sledge became a cart, and the cart became a chariot. A revolution in transport had begun.

This happened about 2000 B.C. Soon the use of the wheel and chariot spread through Asia Minor and reached Mesopotamia. There the knowledge of bronze made it possible for stronger, better wheels to be made.

Bronze and the wheel come to Egypt	About 1750 B.C., a pastoral people came out of Syria, riding in chariots. They were being pushed out of their homes by invaders from Asia, and wanted new lands to live in. They had

heard of the riches of the Nile valley. Armed with bronze weapons, they conquered the delta easily, and ruled Lower Egypt for two hundred years. The Egyptians called them the Hyksos, or the Shepherd Kings.

The Egyptians hated these foreign rulers. From them, however, they learnt about bronze, and also how to make and use the wheel both for transport and for war chariots. Horses were first brought to Egypt at this time.

At last, in 1580 B.C., under a leader called Ahmose from Thebes, the Egyptians drove the Hyksos out. The delta was re-united with Upper Egypt, and Ahmose was made Pharaoh. His dynasty, the eighteenth, began the great period in Egyptian history which is known as the New Kingdom.

The New Kingdom

With their new weapons and knowledge, the Egyptians were now more powerful than ever before. They determined never to be conquered again by the peoples of Asia. With their wheeled chariots they won battle after battle on the open sandy deserts of the Middle East. Under their great kings Tuthmosis I and Tuthmosis III they pushed their rule as far as Mesopotamia.

Never before had Egyptian soldiers been to so far a country. They were amazed when rain fell, and called it 'the Nile in the sky'. They wondered also at the Euphrates River which, unlike the familiar Nile, flowed south instead of north.

The Egyptians now fought with horses and chariots

The Egyptians governed their new empire firmly. Goods of all kinds and slaves from many countries poured into the Nile valley. This was the time when the Hebrew tribes from Palestine, who had settled in Egypt at the time of the Hyksos, began to be persecuted and made to do forced labour. The Book of Exodus describes how they made their escape to Sinai across the Bitter Lakes north of the Gulf of Suez.

Amenhotep IV, called Akhenaten

About 1300 B.C., however, the Pharaohs began to spend more time and money on their luxurious palaces and gardens than on the army and defence. The empire began to crumble.

Things were made worse during the reign of Amenhotep IV, who called himself Akhenaten, 'the believer in the one true God'. He challenged the power of the priests, and declared that it was wrong to think that there were many gods such as Isis, Osiris and Horus in whom the Egyptians had always believed. There was only one true god, said Akhenaten, represented by the disc of the sun. A poet himself, the Pharaoh wrote a hymn to the sun. A lover of art also, he instructed Egyptian artists and sculptors to make people look natural, as they really were, instead of creating the stiff images that had always been customary. The artists obeyed, and pictures of Akhenaten show him with a fat belly and a long chin, playing with his children.

Akhenaten was so occupied with religious reforms and with his family life that he ignored the defence of the empire, which was being attacked by the Hittites in the north. Parts of the empire in Syria and Palestine were lost.

The head of King Akhenaten, carved in stone

The priests were angry. When Akhenaten died, he was succeeded by his nephew Tutankhamen, who was only a boy. The priests were able to regain their power. They, and the later Pharaohs, went back to the old ways. A chance of changing Egyptian life into something new and perhaps better had disappeared.

The last days of Egypt's greatness

The Pharaohs who followed, especially Ramesses II and Ramesses III, were great warriors, and recovered the lands that had been lost. Moreover, they built a fleet of ships. With this navy they captured ports on the Mediterranean coast. Egypt's power was greater than ever before.

Huge temples and palaces lined the banks of the Nile. The temple at Abu Simbel was now built, and the great temple at Karnak, with one hundred and thirty-four columns, each twelve feet thick and sixty-nine feet high, was completed. Enormous statues were made to commemorate the Pharaohs. No more pyramids were built, but large tombs were dug in the hills to the west of the river, where the Pharaohs were buried with quantities of gold ornaments and goods.

This time of greatness, however, was nearing its end. All over the Mediterranean people were travelling and trading. New peoples were coming south from Asia, with new ideas and new energy. One by one, these new peoples cast longing eyes at the Nile valley, with all its wheat and gold.

Four statues of Ramesses II and two of his wife, carved in rock, at Abu Simbel. The door is the entrance to a temple

51

The Iron Age begins

In the north, among the hills of Asia Minor, lived the Hittites. A rough and simple people, about 1100 B.C. they made a great discovery: the hills of Anatolia were rich in iron ore. The Hittites now learnt, perhaps from the people living there before them, how to smelt iron and work it.

Until this time, the metal most commonly used was bronze. But iron has two great advantages over bronze. First, it is much harder, and can be made sharper. Second, iron ore is much more commonly found than copper ore, and people who know about it can have many more tools and weapons. Clearly, a warlike people who knew about iron could quickly become very powerful.

In the north of Mesopotamia was the warrior kingdom of Assur, or Assyria. The Assyrians now learnt about iron from the Hittites. War had always been their life, and society was built around the armies. Great engineers, the Assyrians were skilled at crossing rivers and at building or knocking down city walls. Armed now with iron weapons, they advanced through the Middle East, pillaging and destroying cities and killing their inhabitants.

The conquest of Egypt

Unhappily for the Egyptians, iron was scarce in the Nile valley. They had to import it from Mesopotamia. But the gold mines in Nubia were nearly exhausted. Gold became scarce, and robbers broke into the tombs of the Pharaohs. The price of wheat rose, and the people became discontented.

The Egyptians were therefore unable to resist when the Assyrians, led by the great general, Esarhaddon, invaded the Nile valley in 676 B.C. Esarhaddon conquered Memphis. 'I am powerful, I am all powerful, I am magnificent, I am without an equal among all kings!' he exclaimed. Ten years later the Egyptians rebelled. A new Assyrian army therefore marched farther up the Nile to Upper Egypt, and plundered the great city of Thebes. They broke into the temples and opened up the tombs and stole great quantities of gold and other fine things. It was nearly the end of Egyptian civilization.

The Assyrian Empire did not last long after this, however. The knowledge of iron was spreading, and other peoples were becoming powerful in their turn. First the Babylonians turned on the Assyrians and drove them out. Then the Persians, under their great King, Darius, conquered both Assyria and Babylon, and built an even greater empire. In 525 B.C. the Persian general, Cambyses, marched up the Nile as far as Nubia.

The Persians, in their turn, were overthrown by the Greeks under Alexander the Great (see Chapter 7). In 331 B.C. Alexander's army occupied Egypt, and after his death a line of Greek Pharaohs called Ptolemy ruled the Nile valley. Finally, in 31 B.C., Egypt became a part of the Roman Empire.

Conclusion

The coming of the Iron Age thus brought a time of war and revolution in the Middle East, and finally ended the Egyptian civilization which had lasted three thousand years.

For Africa, also, the Iron Age was of great importance. The knowledge of iron slowly spread southwards to Kush and to the Sudan, as we shall see in a later chapter. As it spread, it changed the life of the African peoples.

Two early Egyptian writings

Thy rising is beautiful on the horizon of heaven, O living Aton!
When thou dawnest on the eastern horizon thou fillest every land with thy beauty.
When thou settest on the western horizon the earth is in darkness in the likeness of death.
Trees and herbage grow green,
Birds flutter in their nests, their wings outstretched in praise to thy spirit.
The fish in the rivers glide to greet thee. . . .

From a hymn to Aton written in the time of Akhenaten

Take that which is set before you. Look not at that which is set before him but at that which lies before you. Laugh when your host laughs. That will be well-pleasing in his heart.
Be not proud because you are learned; but discourse with the ignorant man as with a sage.

From 'An Instruction' by the sage Ptahhotpe in 2650 B.C.

Egyptian Time Chart

Date		Kings	Events
B.C. 4000	PRE-DYNASTIC EGYPT		Growth of small towns in Lower and Upper Egypt. River trade between these towns, using papyrus boats.
3500			
3000			Papyrus used for writing. Hieroglyphic script developed.
	OLD KINGDOM	Narmer	Menes unites the Two Lands.
		Djoser	The Step Pyramid built, 2778.
		Khufu	The Great Pyramids built at Giza.
2500			The Sun Temples to Amon-Re commenced. Expedition to Nubia in 2423. Harkhuf brings pygmy to King Mernere.
2000	MIDDLE KINGDOM		A time of revolutions.
			The Temple at Karnak begun.
		Amenemhet III	The Fayyum made into fertile land, 1850.
		Hyksos Kings	HYKSOS CONQUEST OF EGYPT. Introduction of wheels, chariots and the use of bronze. Hebrews settling in Egypt.
1500	NEW KINGDOM	Ahmose Hatshepsut	Hyksos driven out by Ahmose. Egypt reunited. Trading expedition to Punt on the Red Sea coast. Egyptian Empire extended by Tuthmose I. More temples built. Pharaohs now buried in the Valley of the Kings. Growth of Mediterranean trade. Exodus of Hebrews from Egypt.
		Akhenaten Tutankhamen Seti I Ramesses II Ramesses III	Religious reforms, c. 1372. Temporary decline of empire. Great temples and statues being built, including Abu Simbel near 2nd Cataract. Karnak finished. GREATEST EXTENT OF EGYPTIAN EMPIRE, including much of Mesopotamia.
1000			Demotic script developed.
			Assyrian invasion, 671. ASSYRIAN CONQUEST OF EGYPT, 666.
500	LATE PERIOD	The Ptolemies	Use of iron spreads in the Nile valley. PERSIAN CONQUEST OF EGYPT. GREEK CONQUEST by Alexander the Great, 331.
			Growth of Jebel Barkal, Napata and Meroe on the Upper Nile. Great age of Meroe begins.
A.D.			ROMAN CONQUEST OF EGYPT 31 B.C.

In the last chapter we read how the influence of Egypt spread southward up the Nile.

Even more, however, this influence spread northward into the countries round the Mediterranean Sea. The name of this sea comes from two Latin words, and means 'surrounded by land'. The Mediterranean is like a large lake, open only to the Atlantic Ocean through the Straits of Gibraltar at its western

The Roman Empire at its greatest extent (A.D. 117)

40 20 0 20 40 60

Britannia

Germania

R. Rhine

Gallia

Dacia

R. Danube

BLACK SEA

Hispania

Italia

Rome

Armenia

CASPIAN SEA

Macedonia

Asia

R. Euphrates

R. Tigris

Mauretania

Carthage

Numidia

Africa

Leptis Magna

MEDITERRANEAN SEA

BERBERS

Gadames

Cyrenaica

Memphis

Petra

Egypt

S A H A R A   D E S E R T

'Cart Trail'

'Cart Trail'

Hoggar Mts.

R. Nile

Thebes

ARABIAN DESERT

R. Niger

Nubia

Meroe

RED SEA

NEGROES

Kush

Aksum

HAMITES

Boundary of the
Roman Empire AD 117

Trans-Saharan
trade route

0   500   1000
Miles

40 20 0 20 40 60

A lady of Crete
(from a wall painting)

end. It is a good sea for trade because it has no tides and there are many harbours in its coasts. You can see this from the map. When men learnt to sail ships, ideas and knowledge spread quickly in the Mediterranean.

That is one reason why civilization spread more quickly there than in Africa, which is a huge land mass, and where travel is difficult.

The Egyptians themselves, as we have seen, were not great travellers. They preferred to stay in the valley of the Nile. It is true that they sent ships along the coast and into the Red Sea. These were sent to buy precious goods for the temples and the Pharaoh's palace. It is also true that they pushed their empire into Syria. This was to keep them safe from people in Asia. But most of the time they were happy in the fertile, sunlit valley of the Nile.

Instead of the Egyptians spreading to other places, other people came to Egypt. People came from Palestine and Crete and North Africa. They came to trade, and while they traded they exchanged new ideas.

Crete

Storage jars at the palace of Knossos

Crete is an island in the Mediterranean between Egypt and Greece. The people who lived there learnt to fish and became sailors. Some of their ships went to Egypt, where they sold fish for making purple dye, and copper and olive oil.

From the Egyptians, the Cretans learnt how to build houses out of stone. They built a wonderful palace at Knossos for their king. It had a staircase going up to five levels, there were great halls and many rooms and long corridors. Running water supplied bathrooms. The people produced wonderful works of art. They had other towns at Mycenae in southern Greece and at Troy in Asia Minor.

The Cretans also learnt from the Egyptians how to write, which was essential for traders keeping accounts and ordering supplies.

Phoenicians

The trade between the eastern countries and the Mediterranean passed through the ports of Palestine. One of these ports was a town named Tyre. The people of Tyre became great traders. They controlled towns like Sidon on the Palestine coast, and also the coast of North Africa. The inhabitants of these coastal towns were called Phoenicians.

The Phoenicians were such good sailors that other people used to hire their ships for trade and for making voyages. In this way, they carried goods and ideas around the Mediterranean, and beyond, even as far as Britain. About 500 B.C. an Egyptian Pharaoh sent a Phoenician ship on a trading voyage right round Africa. Of course, he did not know how big Africa was. The voyage took three years. You can read about it in Chapter 13.

The Phoenicians were also good business men. They did not think very much about religion or about life after death, so they did not build great temples; nor are they famous for their art. But they used writing a great deal. They used some Egyptian signs, some Syrian signs, and some from Crete. Traders have to write quickly, for instance when listing the cargo of a ship that is being loaded. To make writing simple and quick, the Phoenicians got rid of most of the signs and kept only twenty-two.

Afterwards the Greeks learnt their writing from the Phoenicians. The Romans learnt theirs from the Greeks. Our own alphabet today is almost the same as the Roman one. You can see how important the Phoenicians were.

In time, Tyre and Sidon were conquered by Egypt, and then by Assyria. The Phoenicians moved their capital to Carthage, near modern Tunis, on the North African coast. The native

57

people living here before the Phoenicians were called *Aperu,* and later known as *Afri.* This is why the Romans called Tunis by the name *Africa.* This name was later given to all of North Africa, and then to the whole continent.

The Greeks

In the last thousand years B.C. there was a lot of trade and travel in the Mediterranean. More people were learning how to build in stone, how to use the wheel, how to work metal, how to weave cotton cloth, how to sail ships, and how to write. They were also talking and arguing, and thinking about all kinds of ideas of how the world was created and how men began, and how people should live together. The most important and creative of all the new people were the Greeks.

The Greeks had arrived from the north, coming from Asia, about 2000 B.C. At first they were a wandering, fighting people. When they reached the sea they fought the Cretans, who had built towns on the mainland, and drove them out. The poems of Homer tell stories of the war against Troy, the Cretan city in Asia Minor.

Statue of a Greek athlete throwing the discus

Although the Greeks fought the Cretans, they also traded with them, and began to learn the arts of civilization. After about 800 B.C., their villages began to grow into towns. They learnt to work in bronze and iron, and to build in stone. Two of their most important towns were Athens and Sparta.

Greece, however, is a mountainous country. High hills divide the valleys from one another. Because of this, the towns did not combine together under one government, but they shared the same language and believed in the same gods. Every fourth year they sent athletes to the games at Olympia, in which only Greeks could compete.

From the Cretans the Greeks learnt writing, and later they invented their own Greek alphabet. After four hundred years they produced great poets and philosophers, artists and sculptors. They loved virtues such as beauty and health, courage, simplicity and moderation.

Democracy

In their towns, or 'city states', the Greeks invented a new system of government. At first they had chiefs, or kings. After a time, however, the kings became too powerful. In most city states there were revolutions, and the kings were driven out. Instead, the Greeks began to elect their rulers. The farmers would come in from the country round about, and they would

The Parthenon at Athens, a Greek temple to the Goddess of Wisdom

all meet in the market place, and vote for their leaders by a show of hands. Any new law had to be approved of by the people. This 'rule by the people' is called *democracy*, a word which in fact comes from the Greek language.

The Greeks were able to do this because they lived in small city states.

Fortunately the Greeks were also brave fighters, because they soon had to defend their freedom in war. When the mighty Persian kings Darius and Xerxes tried to conquer them between 490 and 480 B.C., the Greeks drove them out in a land battle at Marathon and a sea battle at Salamis. Finally they won a great victory at Plataea. The Greeks were very proud of this. Afterwards, some of their finest books and plays were written, and their best temples built.

Soon, however, tragedy came upon them. They began to fight among themselves. A long war between Athens and Sparta left the Greeks so weak and divided that they were easily conquered by King Philip of Macedon, a country in the north.

Alexander the Great

Philip's son was called Alexander. In 336 B.C. he became king of Macedon and Greece. He was a great warrior. He took a Greek army to Asia Minor, and conquered the Persians. Then he invaded Egypt, and made it part of his empire. He built a new city at Alexandria, named after him, which later became a great centre of learning. Finally he marched east, and became ruler of Mesopotamia as well.

Alexander the Great— a portrait in stone

Alexander admired the powerful rulers of the east, whom he had defeated. He wanted to be looked upon as a 'god-king' like the Pharaohs of Egypt and the great kings of Persia. He did not like the democracy of the Greeks. However, in 323 B.C. he fell ill and died in Babylon, while still a young man.

Now his empire split up. It was too large for the Greeks to rule properly. The governors whom Alexander had appointed became rulers of the different parts. The governor of Egypt was a man called Ptolemy. He became the new Pharaoh, and his sons were Pharaohs after him.

For three hundred years, Egypt was ruled by the Ptolemies, until it was conquered by a new power that had grown up in Italy. This was the republic of Rome.

The Romans

When the first Greeks had moved down to the sea from Asia, another tribe of the same race had settled in Italy. After a time, some of them built a town on the banks of the River Tiber, which grew into the powerful city of Rome.

Like the Greeks, the Romans had kings to rule them at first. Like the Greeks, too, they found that their kings became too ambitious and tyrannical. They drove out their last king, Tarquin the Proud, in 510 B.C., and invented a new system of government. The important people of the city elected two leaders called *consuls* to rule them each year. The Romans called this kind of government a *republic*.

A Roman road: the Appian Way near Rome

From Greek traders, the Romans learnt how to write. They invented a new alphabet, even better than that of the Greeks, which is very like ours today. They learnt to build stone houses and temples in the style of the Greeks, and copied their art and stone carving. They believed in the same gods, and wrote stories about them as the Greeks had done.

In character, however, the Romans were different from the Greeks. The Greeks believed in liberty; the Romans believed in order. The Greeks loved beauty and health; the Romans loved power.

The Roman Empire

Statue of a Roman soldier

The Romans became better soldiers than anyone else. Soon their armies brought all Italy under their rule. Then they fought and defeated the Phoenicians of Carthage, and ruled North Africa. Next they conquered Greece and Asia Minor and Egypt. Queen Cleopatra, the last of the Ptolemies, was defeated at the battle of Actium in 31 B.C. Now a Roman governor controlled the valley of the Nile.

Finally the Romans pushed their empire north into Europe as far as the River Danube and the River Rhine. The island of Britain became part of the Roman Empire. The Romans who lived there thought they were on the edge of the world.

The Romans were not only good soldiers: they were especially good at making laws and governing people—not only their own people but those of other countries. When they conquered another country, they ruled its people well, and made them into Roman citizens. They built straight roads between all the towns of the empire. Travellers, traders and government messengers could go where they pleased without fear of being robbed. Soldiers could march quickly from place to place to defend the empire.

However, as a result of these conquests, two great changes came over the Romans. First, their government changed. After 44 B.C., Rome was no longer a republic. It was ruled by one very powerful man, called the Emperor. The first Roman Emperor was Augustus. Now you remember how Alexander the Great had tried to make himself into a kind of god-king. So it was with the Roman Emperors. It was believed that they represented the gods on earth. Temples were built in their honour, and men worshipped there. This idea of the 'god-king' had come, as we know, from Egypt long ago.

Secondly, the Roman people changed from being hard-working and thrifty to being idle, pleasure-seeking and cruel. Slaves poured into Rome from conquered countries. Cruel games were invented. At a great theatre in Rome called the Colosseum, trained slaves called gladiators were made to fight one another or wild animals. The Roman people enjoyed watching people being killed, and thousands went to the arena every day.

Christianity

Soon after the Romans conquered the Middle East, the child Jesus was born among the Hebrew people of Palestine.

When he grew up, Jesus went about telling his people that they must love one another, even their enemies, and so build God's kingdom of love upon earth. His followers came to believe that he was the Christ or Saviour of mankind. The Jewish leaders were jealous of him, however, and put him to death. This was allowed by Pilate, the Roman governor of Palestine.

The followers of Jesus, dismayed for a time, soon recovered. They claimed that Jesus had risen from the dead, that he was the son of God, and that he was still among them. Paul, a leading Jew who had attacked the Christians, was converted to the faith. He travelled through the eastern Mediterranean, teaching about the Christ. He even went as far as Rome.

The Christian communities, or churches, began to grow. At first the Roman government tried to stop them. It was said that the Roman Emperor and the Roman gods must be worshipped, not the God of love the Christians believed in. Many Christians were put to death. However, their numbers continued to increase. After three hundred years, there were so many Christians in all parts of the Empire that even the Emperor himself decided to become a Christian. This Emperor was called Constantine. He was converted in A.D. 325.

The end of the Roman Empire

The Roman Empire lasted for another hundred years after this. Like so many great empires, however, it at last grew weaker. Everywhere there were heavy taxes to support the rich. The poor continued in poverty, while the rich were idle and lived in comfort with slaves to do the work. Officials took bribes, and the government was not trusted. Rival emperors fought against one another.

Meanwhile, barbarian Iron Age tribes began to attack the

empire from the north and east. At first the Roman legions were able to drive them back, but after A.D. 400 there were so many attacks that the Empire was overrun. Even Rome was captured by the Goth tribe. The Vandal tribe plundered Spain, and crossed to North Africa. There they destroyed the towns and farms that the Romans had made.

Fighting to survive, the Romans moved their capital east to Byzantium, which was on the site of modern Istanbul. From here they continued to control Egypt, but their power and influence over most of North Africa was gone. Before we leave this chapter, let us turn back to see what that influence had been.

The Romans in North Africa

The collapse of the Roman Empire in the fifth century ended six hundred years of Roman rule along the North African coast. This rule had begun with the final conquest of Carthage in 146 B.C. (see p. 61), and had been completed with the conquest of Egypt in 31 B.C.

By the time that the Romans ruled North Africa, the Sahara was already a desert. The Romans therefore only settled along the Mediterranean coast. The local inhabitants, Berber and Phoenician, became Roman citizens. Many spoke Latin, and later many became Christian. Some of the greatest early Christian teachers lived and worked in North Africa. St Mark and St Athanasius taught in Alexandria. Later St Augustine, a Berber from Libya, grew up and was educated in Carthage.

The ruins of Leptis Magna, Libya. In the foreground is a theatre

Seventy Roman towns were built in North Africa, and the inhabitants lived ordered, prosperous lives in well-governed provinces which, from east to west, were Egypt, Libya, Africa, Numidia and Mauretania. The coastal climate in the west was very like that of Italy, with a fertile belt of land between the desert and the sea. Here Roman influence was greatest, and the ruins of fine Roman cities like Leptis Magna still stand to remind us of the civilization the Romans created.

Inland, beyond the Atlas Mountains, were more Berbers, but they were nomads, living in tents and herding sheep and goats. They often used to attack the Roman towns and rob them, so the Romans set up military posts quite far inland. The farthest south was at the oasis of Fezzan. However, the Romans made no attempt to rule the interior.

Roman pillars at Leptis

Of course, we know from the 'cart paintings' (p. 80) that trading expeditions used to cross the desert to the Niger. A Roman coin has been picked up on the banks of the Niger near Timbuktu. However, this does not mean that Roman traders went there. The Berbers controlled the desert trails, and their power increased after the camel arrived in North Africa about A.D. 500. By that time the Roman Empire was breaking up.

Farther east, however, lay the rich valley of the Nile. The Romans used Egypt, one of their most valuable provinces, as a giant granary. Every year grain and gold poured into Rome and other cities of the empire. The Egyptians gained from Roman administration, but their farming was damaged beyond repair.

The Romans were content to control the lower Nile valley. Puzzled by the mystery of the Nile, they sent expeditions to explore up-river, but these never reached very far. They took gold from Nubia, but in spite of occasional fights they did not try to conquer Kush, with its capital at Meroe, about which we shall read in the next chapter.

After the break-up of the empire, the eastern Emperors at Byzantium continued to rule Egypt until it was conquered by the Moslems in A.D. 641.

8 Meroe

In vain the Egyptians had tried to resist the invaders from the north. The great armies of the Assyrians, as we read in Chapter 6, had iron weapons. So too had the hosts of the Persians who followed. It was the end of old Egypt. For more than two thousand years the quiet valley of the Nile, its temples crumbling in the sun, was to be ruled by foreign powers.

Egypt's loss was to be Africa's gain. When the Assyrians came, many Egyptians moved away to the south. There they would be able to keep their worship of the sun god Amon-Re and their other customs and beliefs.

First they went to Nubia. Already there had been Egyptian colonies in Nubia for a long time, for the gold mines there were the richest in the world. Sometimes Nubia had been more powerful than Egypt itself. But the Assyrians wanted Nubia for its gold. Some of the Egyptians left the country to move even farther up the Nile.

Here, where the rivers from the Ethiopian highlands, today called the Atbara and the Blue Nile, join the main river, was the land of Kush. The country was called by this name because the people living there were once related to the Kushites of Ethiopia. These, again, were Hamites from Arabia. They were supposed to be descended from Kush, the son of Ham, the son of Noah, whose story is in the Book of Genesis and the Koran. In fact Negroes from the Sudan had long been mixing with the Hamites in this country, and the people of Kush were mostly a Negro African people.

For a long time Kush had been a province of Egypt. The principal town was at Napata. When the Egyptian Empire grew weaker about 1000 B.C., Kush became independent, ruled by its own kings. Then in about 700 B.C. the Kushite king, called Kashta, conquered Egypt and became its Pharaoh. So for a time the Pharaohs of Egypt were Africans from Kush.

It was in the reign of Kashta's great-grandson, Tanwetamani, that the Assyrians conquered Egypt. Kush was now once more a small kingdom far up the Nile.

Meroe

At first the Kushites continued to have their capital at Napata. Later they moved it up-river to Meroe, which is not far from present-day Khartoum.

The Nile valley in the time of Meroe

There were good reasons for choosing Meroe. Firstly it was on the trade route from the Sudan to Ethiopia. Secondly the land was good for farming. Today Meroe is a ruin in the desert, but at that time there was more rain. Every year the Nile flooded over its banks. Indeed, this fertile land between the Nile and the Atbara was known as 'the island of Meroe', where grass grew and planted trees could flourish.

Thirdly there was iron ore. Although the Kushites wanted to keep their Egyptian customs and beliefs, they had not neglected to learn valuable things from the Assyrians. Above all they had learnt how to smelt and use iron. Iron ore was scarce in the Lower Nile valley. At Meroe there were rich supplies in the ground.

Now this new kingdom of Kush, or Meroe, became more wealthy and important. A large city of brick houses was built. The kings and queens lived in a stone palace of many rooms surrounding an open courtyard. When they died, they were buried in pyramids after the Egyptian custom. However, these pyramids were smaller than the Egyptian ones, and more pointed in shape, as you can see in the picture. The tomb of King Tanwetamani, which is still standing today, had a painted blue ceiling with gold stars on it. In the tomb were placed things which would be useful to the dead king in the next life. When the king died, some of his servants were put to death to accompany him. Little model figures, to represent these servants, were then placed in the king's tomb beside him.

Religion, as we have seen, was important to the people of

The pyramids of Meroe

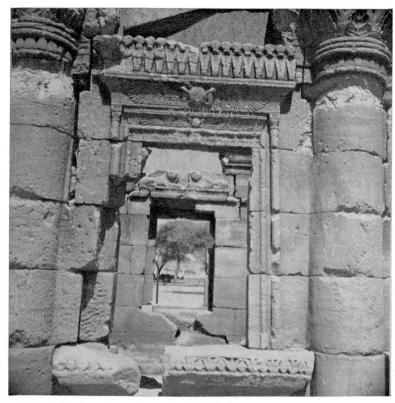

Meroe. Many temples were built, some of which we can still see today. The largest was the temple to Amon-Re at Jebel Barkal. There was also a temple to Amon-Re at Meroe itself, built in the Egyptian style. Its sandstone pillars were carved with pictures of gods and of kings and queens. Its rooms were painted in bright colours. A line of stone rams led up to the entrance. Another temple, at Naqa, a few miles from Meroe, had arches and pillars of the Roman style. This shows that although the Romans never conquered Meroe, the Kushites were learning from them also. In their temples, however, the Kushites worshipped not only Egyptian gods, but also some gods of their own. The most important of these was the lion god Apedemak.

Art in Meroe

The people of Meroe were great artists. They made statues of their kings, like that of King Netekamani. They painted pictures on the walls of the temples. They made fine jewellery such as bracelets, necklaces and ear-rings of gold and coloured stone. They made beautiful vases and pots of clay and bronze, and painted pictures on the outside.

The people of Meroe also knew how to write. At first they used Egyptian writing in the Egyptian language. After a time, however, they began to write in their own African language. They also changed the symbols and even invented their own 'cursive' or joined script. We do not yet know what their language was, and so we cannot understand the writing, although Meroitic script is so like Egyptian. When scholars can interpret this writing, we shall know much more about Meroe and Kush.

The great age of Meroe

The greatest days of Meroe lasted from about 250 B.C. to about A.D. 100. During that time the inhabitants of Meroe fought successful wars against people round about. We do not know who these enemies were, but wall pictures show long lines of captives kneeling bound before the king.

Made bold by success, the Queen or Candace of Meroe in 21 B.C. decided to raid Egypt, which had been conquered by the Romans ten years before. The Roman governor, Petronius, was angry at this attack. Two years later he sent an army south to Napata, and plundered it in revenge. After that there was usually peace in the Nile valley. The Romans never conquered Meroe, which was too far from their base in the delta, but they sent more than one expedition beyond Meroe to explore the Upper Nile.

The wealth of Meroe depended on trade, and above all on its production of iron. At first the Kushites had not known about iron. Herodotus, the Greek historian, wrote in 430 B.C. that their prisoners were bound in gold chains, their weapons had stone points, and bronze was a rare metal. Now, learning from the Assyrians, the people of Meroe mined the ore, smelted the iron, sold it and grew wealthy. Huge piles of slag from the smelting have been found near the ruined town. Iron was eagerly sought by the people of Ethiopia, the peoples of the Sudan and the inhabitants of the Nile valley. A stone quay was built at Meroe for the river boats that sailed up the Nile.

Iron-working spreads through Africa

Meroe was a good place for this trade, because the Nile could be crossed there. Many people passed through Kush between east and west as well as between north and south. Hamitic

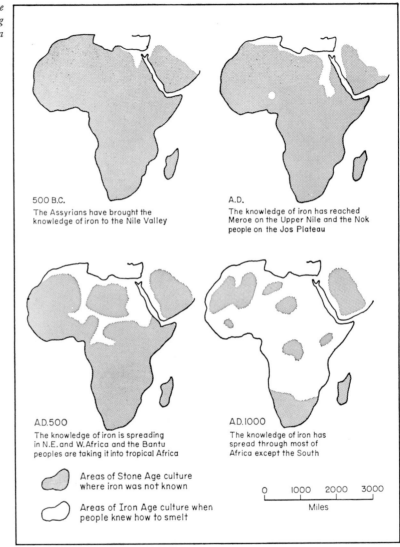

*How the knowledge
of iron-working
spread through Africa*

500 B.C.
The Assyrians have brought the
knowledge of iron to the Nile Valley

A.D.
The knowledge of iron has reached
Meroe on the Upper Nile and the Nok
people on the Jos Plateau

A.D.500
The knowledge of iron is spreading
in N.E. and W.Africa and the Bantu
peoples are taking it into tropical Africa

A.D.1000
The knowledge of iron has
spread through most of
Africa except the South

Areas of Stone Age culture
where iron was not known

Areas of Iron Age culture when
people knew how to smelt

0   1000   2000   3000

Miles

peoples of Ethiopia were mixing with the Negro peoples of the
Sudan. Gradually the knowledge of iron-working, and of gold
and copper, spread from Meroe to the other peoples of the
Sudan, and so to tropical Africa.

First, this knowledge spread westward to Darfur. From there
it passed to the Sao people of Lake Chad, and to the Negro

people of the Benue and Niger Rivers. A few of the Niger people already knew how to smelt iron, however. The Nok people (see p. 79) were perhaps smelting iron as early as 300 B.C. They had learnt about it from Berber traders across the Sahara.

After this, it was not long before the knowledge of iron reached the new Bantu-speaking people of the Cameroons. By them it was taken southward into Central Africa. At last the long centuries of the Stone Age in Africa were coming to an end.

Everywhere the method of smelting iron was the same as that used by the people of Meroe. The furnace was made of clay. The bellows for blowing the fire consisted of a hollow wooden drum, with a leather bag attached to the end. The method was a strictly guarded secret, controlled by the king.

New customs also spread

People who used iron were stronger in war than people who used stone. When they conquered, they ruled. When they ruled, they imposed new customs.

In this way, customs and ideas from Meroe spread across the Sudan to West Africa. Some of them spread into the southern and eastern part of Africa as well. But the customs of Meroe were descended from those of Egypt. That is why old Egypt is so important in the history of Africa.

Some of these customs and ideas will be mentioned later in this book. Let us stop to consider one or two of them now.

The most important was the idea of the god-king. The later Egyptians had believed that the king was a kind of god, with special powers. Each year he must hoe the first plot, sow the first seed, cast the first metal. This custom spread through Africa, and is even observed by some tribal chiefs today. Again, because the king was supposed to be a god, ordinary people were not allowed to see him eating food. This custom came to be observed in the Sudan by the Zaghawa chiefs and, for example, by the Alafin of Oyo in the Niger forest.

We have read how, when the Pharaoh of Egypt died, many of his servants as well as his cattle had to be killed in order to accompany him on his journey into the next world. So in West Africa it became the custom for slaves to die when their king or master died. In the south, for example among the Bemba of Zambia, it was the rule that many people must be sacrificed upon the death of a chief.

Customs like these were found in strong kingdoms like Oyo, Benin, Ghana, Baluba or Monomotapa's empire. Indeed, the idea of having strong kings came from the kingdom of the Nile. Other African peoples were not reached by these ideas. The Bantu of the Zambezi valley and of East Africa, and the Negroes of the west coast rain forest lived in small village communities and did not have strong kings to unite them.

Other beliefs that spread from Meroe were about religion. The Egyptians had made pictures of their gods with the bodies of men but with the heads of animals. In Meroe the god Amon-Re was believed to have the head of a ram. Later we find that the Mandingo people of West Africa gave their god of thunder the head of a ram. Shango, the national god of the Yoruba, also had a ram's head. Of course the African peoples had their own stories about their own pagan gods, but we can sometimes see the influence of Meroe and the kingdoms of the Nile.

The decline of Meroe

These are some of the reasons why Meroe was so important for the history of Africa. Long before these influences had spread through Africa, however, the Kingdom of Meroe had disappeared.

After about A.D. 150 Meroe began to grow poorer and weaker. There were three reasons for its decline. One was that trade was decreasing. The biggest trade had always been with Egypt, whether under the Persians, or the Greeks, or the Romans. When the Roman Empire began to grow weaker, disorder spread, and the demand for iron and gold fell away.

Secondly, the climate was becoming drier. The desert was advancing, and it was difficult to grow enough food.

Lastly there was the growing power of Aksum in the Ethiopian highlands. The Kushites of Meroe had unwisely raided Aksum from time to time, taking away plunder and captives. In A.D. 325 King Ezana of Aksum waged a war of crushing revenge. The towns of Meroe were burnt down, statues were pulled to the ground, trees were uprooted. Stores were looted or thrown into the Nile, and those people who escaped death fled across the river to the west. Some people believe that the royal family escaped to Darfur, but this may never be known for certain. Meroe and its daughter towns, at least, were now desolate. Their ruins were left to the advancing desert and to the erosion of time.

The destruction of Meroe

Through the might of the Lord of All, I took the field against the
    people of Noba . . . when they
Without consideration slew their neighbours and plundered our
    envoys and our messengers
Whom I had sent to interrogate them, robbing them of their pos-
    sessions and
Seizing their spears. When I sent again and they did not hear me,
    and reviled me
And made off, I took the field against them.

Prisoners and booty were brought back by my people who marched
    out; while I burnt their towns,
Those of masonry and those of straw, and seized their corn and
    their bronze and the dried meat
And the images in the temples, and destroyed the stocks of corn
    and cotton; and (the enemy)
Plunged into the River Seda (Nile), and many perished in the
    water,
The number I know not; and as their vessels foundered, a multitude
    of people,
Men and women, were drowned. . . .

My people returned safe and sound . . . after they had seized their
    booty through the power of the Lord of Heaven.
And I erected a throne at the junction of the Rivers Seda and
    Takkaze,
Opposite the town of masonry which is on this peninsula.

A report of King Ezana's war
against Kush, A.D. *325*

9 The Negroes

So far in this book, we have read how civilization spread out-wards from Egypt and from the Fertile Crescent of lands that stretch from Palestine to Mesopotamia. It extended west to the Mediterranean countries, and south to Meroe; but it did not yet reach the rest of Africa.

In the next two chapters we shall see why this was so. We shall also read about the other peoples in the rest of Africa, whom civilization did not yet reach.

It is difficult to say just what 'civilization' is. Clearly it has

The migration of peoples in Africa

much to do with living in towns and cities. When people come together in large numbers, they work out a system of laws and ideas of right and wrong. In daily life people have different tasks, so that each individual can become very good at his own special task. Many arts develop, such as building, sculpture, painting and music. Knowledge and wisdom are shared, and ideas about life after death are discussed.

The importance of trade and travel

If you think about it, you will realize that civilization can only develop in a country where some people can grow more food than they need. Then they can sell to people who are doing other work like building, or trading, or teaching, or studying. If each family can only just grow enough food for itself, the village cannot become a town, and civilization cannot grow. On the other hand, if the family just manages to feed itself by hunting and by collecting wild fruits in the forest, the people cannot make the effort to learn new ways of living.

Moreover, civilization can only develop where there is a good trade route. Then the town or country which has more than one kind of produce, like grain, gold, metal, or hides, can sell some of it to another town or country which produces something different. As a result, both become wealthier. They can employ builders and engineers and writers, and become a civilized people.

You have probably noticed that each of the early civilizations we have been reading about started on a river, or by the sea. Sumer was on the River Euphrates, and Egypt was on the Nile. The Chinese civilization began on the Hwang Ho. Crete is an island in the sea, and the Greeks also lived by the sea. Living by water, these peoples made boats. Boats helped trade, because they could carry heavier loads than a man, or a pack animal, or even a wheeled cart. Nor did it cost money to move the boats, because they had sails.

Difficulty of trade in Africa

Africa has great rivers, but on only one of them, the Nile, did a great civilization begin. Why not elsewhere? Firstly, because only the Nile had annual floods which brought down soil from the mountains. Secondly, because all the others—the Niger, the Congo and the Zambezi, for example—flowed into oceans which were thousands of miles away from the early civilizations of the Mediterranean, from which people could learn.

The Tisisat Falls on the Blue Nile, Ethiopia

Thirdly, because all these rivers had rapids or waterfalls which prevent boats sailing far up them. This is because Africa is like a great tableland, or plateau. Rivers flow over the edge of the plateau to the sea in a series of steps, or escarpments. The Niger, on the other hand, has a delta of small mouths through which it is difficult for boats to find their way.

Moreover, Africa is a huge mass of land. Most of it is far from the sea. Travel was always difficult, many kinds of wild animal made life dangerous, and tropical diseases threatened visitors from other lands.

Lastly, there was the great barrier presented by the Sahara Desert. For a long time, the Sahara had been growing more and more dry. People from the Mediterranean, where civilization was advancing, could no longer make the journey to the south so easily. They had to travel for many weeks through hot, dry country, in great danger from thirst and, sometimes, from brigands. Parts of the Sahara were soft sand. Wheeled carts could no longer pass through. Even horses and mules would die. Not till the camel came to North Africa from Arabia in about A.D. 500 could trade begin again in a small way. By that time, the Roman Empire was collapsing. The Arab empires in North Africa did not begin till after A.D. 650.

Camels crossing the desert   Even the few travellers who did manage to cross the desert found that the lands to the south were hot and uncomfortable to live in compared with their own countries.

For these reasons, the peoples who lived south of the Sahara, in what is called tropical Africa, did not advance so far in civilization. But they did not stand still. In spite of all the difficulties, some trade reached them. With it came some knowledge from the rest of the world. Meanwhile they, on their own, made their own discoveries. In some parts of Africa great kingdoms, some of them well organized and governed, grew up. We shall read of these in later chapters.

First, however, let us look at the peoples who were living in tropical Africa at about the time of the fall of Meroe in A.D. 325.

Pygmies and Bushmen   The oldest inhabitants of Africa were small people rather like the Bushmen and Pygmies of today.

Pygmy-type people and Negrilloes lived in the rain-forest areas of West Africa and the Congo. They were probably descended from the Sangoan men of the Middle Stone Age about whom we read in Chapter 2. They did not build proper houses, but lived in shelters made from leaves and branches. They collected their food in the forest, and did not know how to farm.

The same was true of the Bushman-type people who lived all the way from the highlands of East Africa to the Cape. They were descended from the Stillbay people of the Middle Stone Age. They hunted with bows and arrows, and lived in the open, sometimes using caves and rock shelters. We have read in Chapter 3 how they used to make drawings on the cave walls.

Some descendants of these people are still alive today. Their races are the oldest in Africa, perhaps the oldest in the world.

Negroes

The Negroes are a different people. For a long time before the kingdom of Meroe, Negroes had been living in West Africa between the desert and the sea. We do not know where they came from. Either they grew out of the Sangoan Stone Age people, or they came from the east about twenty thousand years ago. If they came from the east, they must have sprung from the Stone Age peoples of southern Asia.

We think that the Negroes may have come from Asia because most West African tribes have old stories that their forefathers came from the east. Secondly, scientists have found that some Negro blood is like that of people in northern India. Lastly, Negroes are much taller than the Negrilloes and Bushmen.

But we still do not know for certain. The skull of a Negro, dating back over ten thousand years, has been dug up near Khartoum. Another, of about the same age, has been found at Timbuktu. This tells us that Negroes were living in the grasslands of the Sudan and the Sahara between 10,000 and 5,000 years ago.

Mostly the Negroes liked rivers where they could find fish, and clay for making pots, so they lived on the banks of the Niger, around Lake Chad and along the Shari River. Others lived beside the Upper Nile. A few lived in the Sahara itself, where streams and rivers also used to flow. Perhaps they made the wonderful paintings on the rock walls of the Hoggar hills.

Negroes leave the Sahara

The Negroes who had been living by the rivers and wells of the Sahara grasslands were now driven south by two enemies.

The first enemy was the slow drying up of the desert. Partly the result of the changing climate, this was also caused by the newly-arrived herds of nomadic tribes. As the knowledge of keeping sheep and goats began to spread from Asia, these flocks and herds began to graze and over-graze the shrinking grasslands. Sand and stones replaced the grass. The rivers and springs dried up.

These newly-arrived nomadic tribes were the second enemy of the Negroes. They were Hamitic people who had crossed from Asia to Africa about 5000 B.C. Some of them, as we have seen, settled in the Nile valley. Out of these settlements had grown the Egyptian civilization. Others, however, pushed on past the Tibesti Plateau to Lake Chad. Others again moved along the Mediterranean coast. There they formed the Berber peoples who now wandered south across the Hoggar ranges.

Leaving the Sahara, the Negroes now lived mostly in the grasslands south of the desert, which we call the Sudan. Others settled in the forest of the Lower Niger, driving out the Negrilloes who lived there.

In the east, however, Negroes met the peoples of the Nile valley, and fought with the Egyptians. By 1000 B.C. Negroes were found among the governors, officials and soldiers of the Egyptian Empire. Negroes played an important part in the Kingdom of Meroe from 600 B.C. to A.D. 300.

The Nok culture

At first the civilization of Meroe did not reach the peoples of the Western Sudan. On the Jos Plateau of Northern Nigeria, however, Negroes made their own progress. Perhaps they were influenced by trade with Berbers in the north.

We call the development of these people the Nok culture, named after the village of Nok, near Jos. In recent years, tin miners at Nok found some model heads made of baked clay, or terra cotta. The most famous is that of a Negro woman. Other heads and parts of statues were soon found at other places round about. There were also stone hoes, showing that these people had started simple farming. The discovery of an iron

Early migrations into West Africa

Knowledge of iron from North Africa 400 B.C.

10   0   10   20

Rock paintings 500 B.C.

20   20

Niger R.

L.Chad

Knowledge of iron from Meroe 100 B.C.

10   10

NOK CULTURE AFTER 900 B.C.

Benue R.

BANTU PEOPLES FORMING A.D. 0–500

Land over 3000ft

Berber migration southward from N.Africa

Slow movement of Negroes from the east after 10,000B.C.

0   500

Miles

10   0   10   20

A terracotta head from Nok

Saharan trade routes

axe-head shows that these people also knew how to smelt iron.
We believe that the Nok culture lasted from about 900 B.C.
to about A.D. 200.

By about 100 B.C., trade between the Jos Plateau and Meroe
passed along regular routes. Trade routes also crossed the
Sahara from the Berber peoples of the north, now partly ruled
by the Roman Empire. The later rock-paintings, on rock walls
in the Hoggar Mountains, show that wheeled carts were in
use on these long, dusty trails.

As the desert dried up, parts of it became deep sand, and
wheels could no longer be used. Trade declined during Roman
times. A Roman coin has been picked up on the banks of the
Upper Niger, but otherwise there is little sign of Roman influence south of the Sahara. Trade might have stopped altogether.
Then the camel was brought to Africa from Arabia in the fifth

century A.D. The trade routes were opened once more.

These trade routes were later very important in the growth of the Negro kingdoms of the Sudan. You can see the most important ones on the map. Starting in the east, the Selima trail from Egypt led to Darfur and Wadai. The Bilma trail from Libya went to Bagirmi and Bornu. Farther west the Ghadames trail from Carthage (modern Tunis) led straight to the Middle Niger plateau, where the Nok people lived. Lastly, farther west, the Taodeni trail linked Morocco with the Upper Niger, where the kingdom of Ghana later grew.

The Negro peoples of the western Sudan gained from a double influence. From the Hamitic Berbers in the north they learnt to farm and trade, and perhaps how to work gold. From Meroe on the Nile they gained ideas of kingship, government and religious belief. From both the Berbers and Meroe they learnt how to smelt iron.

The Guinea Coast

Meanwhile the Negroes who had been pushed south into the forest region were not reached by these influences until later. By A.D. 1000, however, they too had the knowledge of iron, farming and trade. Great kingdoms were to grow here also. We shall read about these in later chapters.

10 Hamites, Nilotes and Bantu

The Negroes, about whom we read in the last chapter, were one of two important groups of peoples in northern Africa ten thousand years ago. The other group was the brown-skinned, straight-nosed and long-haired people whom we call the Hamites.

The Hamites have been given this name because, according to an old story, they were descended from the family of Ham, one of the sons of Noah whom we read about in the Koran and the Book of Genesis. They first came to Africa from Arabia about ten thousand years ago.

Some of these early Hamites settled in the Nile valley. We have seen how, after a long time, they made the Egyptian civilization. Others went to live in the highlands of Ethiopia, where they kept sheep and cattle. They lived in tents and moved from place to place. We call such people 'nomads'. From time to time they were joined by more Hamites from across the Red Sea.

The Sidama

About 200 B.C., a new wave of Hamites came across the sea to Ethiopia. One reason for this invasion was that the Arabian desert was becoming very dry, and there was more rain in the highlands of Ethiopia. Another reason was the conquest of Arabia by the Persians, whose great empire now spread throughout the Middle East.

When this happened, some of the early Hamites who already lived in Ethiopia were driven westward. A leading tribe among them was the Sidama.

The Sidama were a cattle-owning people. They loved their cattle, with their high backs and great, long horns. Cattle were almost as important to them as the Nile had been to the ancient Egyptians. They had many rules about how their cattle should be treated. No man could kill a cow for food, but the blood of a live animal could be taken to drink. The Sidama drank milk, but this milk could not be boiled. Some time had to pass, after milking, before it could be consumed. It was wrong to drink milk out of a clay pot, and wooden bowls and gourds were used.

The Sidama were a strong fighting people. They met Negro settlers, and drove them back towards the Nile. They also drove

Long-horned cattle

out the early Hamites who had been in that part of Ethiopia before them.

Early Hamites in East Africa

These early Hamites who had been driven out by the Sidama wandered southward, taking their cattle with them. Some of them settled in the area now known as Kenya and northern Tanzania, where they lived for a thousand years.

Some went down to the east coast, where they built fishing villages and towns, like Rhapta (see Chapter 13).

Others stayed on the plateau, wandering with their herds. Slowly they settled down. In their old homes, among the rocky highlands of Ethiopia, they had been accustomed to building stone walls. Now, living along the Rift Valley of East Africa, they again built their homes on the hillsides. They used to make a hut by digging a hollow in a steep slope, and protecting it with a wall on the lower side. The entrance was through a gap in the stone wall.

Remains of old dwellings like these have been found in the Nandi and Uasin Gishu districts of Kenya. Farther south at Engaruka, near Lake Eyasi in the Rift Valley of Tanzania, there are the remains of a town consisting of about six thousand ruined stone houses and three miles of stone terracing on the hillside. These ruins may not be more than five hundred years old, but they were built by the descendants of the early Hamites, who still lived in Tanzania until they were driven out by the Masai.

Early Hamites in Southern Africa

A few of the early Hamites went even farther south, and crossed the Zambezi. Here some of them married with the Bushman

Hamitic warriors of the Sudan

people and formed the Hottentots, who later moved slowly across Southern Africa as far as the Cape.

It may have been an early Hamite or Hottentot clan who lived in the fortified rocks south of the Limpopo. One of these, called Mapungubwe, had a flat top about a hundred yards long, and vertical sides too steep to climb, except in one place. On the top are ancient stone walls, and the skeletons of buried people. Lying with the skeletons, when they were found thirty years ago, were some gold ornaments. There were also wooden carvings of animals that had been covered with thin sheets of gold; the wood has rotted away, but the gold has been left.

Others of the early Hamites stayed in Mashonaland. Perhaps they were the first people there to use stone for building cattle kraals. They were still living there when the Karanga arrived in the eleventh century.

The Karanga were a Bantu tribe. Before we come to the Bantu, however, we must first look at the formation of one other African people, the Nilotes.

Nilotes

Let us go back to the Nile, far to the north. It is the first century A.D., and the kingdom of Meroe is still flourishing. To the south, along the White Nile and the Bahr-el-Gazal, were living together Negro clans and some of those Sidama who had driven them out of their homes on the Upper Nile. Gradually these groups intermarried, and formed a new people whom we call the Nilotes. The Nilotes were, and still are today, very like the Negroes to look at, being tall and very dark-skinned. But they had many Hamitic customs and beliefs, especially about cattle.

Their religious ideas may have come from Meroe. The Shilluk, an important Nilotic tribe, believed that their chief, or king, was one of the gods. This 'divine king' was not allowed to die naturally, but was put to death when he became old. Then his spirit, so it was thought, could pass alive to the new king.

Another Nilotic tribe in the Sudan is the Dinka. In Uganda the Acholi, and in Kenya the Luo are both Nilotic peoples.

A Dinka tribesman

Bantu

Finally we come to the Bantu, who today inhabit a huge area of Central and Southern Africa.

After the first Hamites had come down from the highlands of Ethiopia to the Nile, some of them crossed the river and migrated right across the Sudan until they reached the Negroes

Bantu woman making cooking utensils

in the Cameroons. We do not know when this happened, but it was before the time of the Nilotes. Probably it was before the time of Meroe, and even before the Assyrian conquest of Egypt.

Once again, there was a mixing of people—mainly of Hamites and Negroes. Different tribes were formed. They lived the lives of simple farmers on the grasslands of the Cameroon Highlands.

As time went on, the tribes spoke different languages; yet they were the same kind of language. Similar words happened in each one. All languages had the same word for 'man'—*umuntu*. So also in the plural, the word for 'men' or 'people' was everywhere the same—*abantu*.

This language is different from the language of the Negroes of the west; different from that of the Hamites of Ethiopia; different even from that of the Nilotes, who were also a mixed people. The tribes who spoke the 'umuntu-abantu' languages were therefore another district 'family' of people. One of the first Europeans who came to Africa a hundred years ago, finding that they were a separate people, decided to give them the name of *Bantu*, because that is the word they all use.

The Bantu move away

After a long time, perhaps five hundred years, so that it was about the beginning of the Christian era, the knowledge of how to make iron reached the early Bantu in the Cameroons from Meroe. Now they were able to use iron hoes, and so to grow more food, and the population began to increase.

Good land, however, was becoming scarcer in the Sudan. All the time the rain was becoming less, and the dry sands of the Sahara were creeping south. Tribes began to fight about land.

When this happened, some tribes decided to migrate and find new countries.

New lands

It was not easy to find new land that was good. First, of course, it had to be fertile for growing crops. The food grown by early Bantu farmers was mainly yams and plantain. Second, there had to be iron ore in the ground. A tribe with iron was stronger than one without. A tribe without iron had to buy from another tribe. Third, there had to be salt. People and cattle need salt with their food to be healthy and strong. Sometimes people had to make salt from grass; but it was better to find a place where it was already in the rock.

A fourth need was particularly for those tribes which had

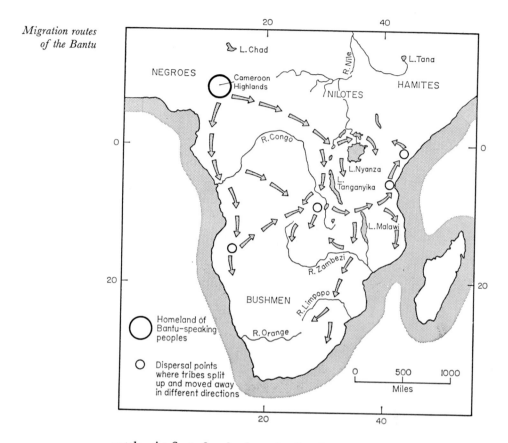

cattle. At first, few had cattle. In time, as they met the Nilotes
and Hamites in the north-east, more Bantu tribes learned how
to keep cattle. Now they found before long that in large parts of
Africa there is an enemy of cattle. This is the tsetse-fly. Tsetse
brings disease which always kills cattle, and sometimes people.
Cattle-owning Bantu had to find tsetse-free country to settle in.

Most of the Bantu were Sudan people, from grasslands, not
forest people. As they moved south, they kept to the highlands
where there was more grassland and the trees were well-spaced.
Most of them avoided the thicker forest of the Congo basin,
although some went to live there.

**Routes taken by the
Bantu**

There were two main routes followed by the migrating Bantu.
You can see them on the map. Some tribes went south along

the west coast to Angola, and then moved across the Congo highlands to Lake Tanganyika. These were mostly tribes without cattle, who followed the custom that the son inherits from the mother.

Others moved across the Sudan to the region of the great lakes and the Rift Valley, and after a time moved south from there. These were mostly cattle-owning tribes, who followed the custom that the son inherits from the father. Taking a more easterly route, they mixed more with the early Hamites about whom we read at the beginning of this chapter.

The Bantu migration was a great event in African history. It brought the Iron Age and the knowledge of agriculture south of the equator, and peopled the southern part of the continent as far as the Drakensberg Mountains with a new and vigorous branch of the human race.

11 Ethiopia

While these new peoples, about whom we have read in the last chapter, were forming and beginning to migrate across Africa, great events were taking place in the east, north and west of the continent. We shall first look at the story of Ethiopia in the north-eastern highlands.

We have seen that, when the Roman Empire collapsed, the kingdom of Meroe on the Upper Nile also declined.

There were two other reasons for the decline of Meroe. One was the changing climate. The desert was becoming drier, and food was difficult to produce. The other reason was the growing power of Aksum in the Ethiopian highlands.

Aksum

The people of Ethiopia were of both Hamitic and Semitic stock. For centuries, since as long ago as 5000 B.C., they had come in small numbers across the Red Sea. In the highlands above the hot, dry coast the climate was pleasant, and refreshing rain fell upon grass-covered hillsides.

The earliest settlers were Hamitic nomads, with dark brown skins, straight noses and black hair. They were known to the Egyptians as Kushites. They wandered on the plateau with their flocks and herds.

Mountains and valleys of Ethiopia

The Kingdom of Aksum
A.D. 300 to 800

Later, about 700 B.C., more people began to come from Arabia, partly because of the Persian conquest. Among them were Semitic traders from South Arabia, with light brown skins rather like the Arabs of today. In those times, many boats sailed the Red Sea and the Persian Gulf (see Chapter 12). The South Arabian merchants were sometimes as wealthy as the Phoenicians in the Mediterranean.

On the fertile plateau of Ethiopia, these traders found gum, spices and even ivory. They made ports on the coast, of which the biggest was Adulis. Inland they made colonies. The greatest centre was the town of Aksum. 'To Aksum', wrote a Greek trader, 'all the ivory is brought from the country beyond the Nile.'

By A.D. 300, Aksum was the capital of a great kingdom. The ruler of the city held power as far as the Red Sea coast to the east and as far as the Upper Nile in the west. Even the kingdom of Meroe was soon to be overthrown.

Ezana the king

The greatest king of Aksum was Ezana. He ruled from about 300 to 330. His scribes wrote accounts in Greek and Arabic script of his wars against Arabia, and against the peoples of the Upper Nile. At the end of Chapter 8 we read how he sent an army down the Atbara to destroy Meroe in 325.

In order to commemorate his victories, Ezana ordered his stone masons to put up tall stone monuments. Such monuments are called 'obelisks'. The largest obelisk at Aksum was over one hundred feet high. Several are still standing there today. It is no wonder that Ezana was given a long royal title, naming the countries which he ruled, and ending with the words 'King of Kings, son of Mars the Unconquered'.

Perhaps the greatest event of Ezana's reign, however, was his conversion to Christianity.

Christianity in Ethiopia

For three hundred years since the journeys of St Paul, the Christian Church had grown slowly in the countries of the Mediterranean. Sometimes, especially under the Emperor Diocletian in 300, Christians had been cruelly persecuted by the Romans. Then, as we read in Chapter 7, there was a great change. The Emperor Constantine made Christianity the accepted religion of the Roman Empire. Later, he himself became a Christian. After this happened, the Church grew rapidly.

Obelisk at Aksum

At this time, traders from Aksum were often in Egypt. Christians in Alexandria heard about Ezana and his empire. Before long some missionaries made the journey southward to Ezana's court. King Ezana listened to them, and soon became a Christian, with other members of his court. He now changed his title, leaving out 'son of Mars'. Instead he was king of Aksum and other countries 'with the help of the Lord of Heaven and Earth'.

As the years passed, more and more people in Ethiopia were converted. Seventy years after Ezana had died, two Christian Syrians from Tyre, who were brothers, came to Aksum and built the first church there. One of them, Frumentius, went to Alexandria to be consecrated the first Bishop of Aksum by St Athanasius in 402. He then returned to Ethiopia and stayed there for the rest of his life.

Because Aksum was so far away from the Mediterranean, however, the Christians in Aksum developed customs and beliefs which were rather different from those of the Roman Church in the west and the Byzantine Church in the east.

Local languages were used instead of Latin, and different festivals were held. These variations have continued to the present day.

Ethiopia cut off by Islam

Two hundred years after Ezana, the Church and people of Aksum became even more isolated. The reason for this was the sudden rise of the Islamic Empire, which is described in Chapter 1 of Book Two. In 641, nine years after the death of Mohammed, the Arab armies conquered Egypt from the feeble Byzantine Empire.

As we shall see, when the Moslems conquered Egypt, they allowed the Christian Church to continue there. They tried but failed to conquer Christian Nubia, and they left Aksum alone for the time being. As a result, Christianity continued in Ethiopia, whose church kept in touch with the 'Coptic' Church of Egypt.

Apart from this contact, however, Aksum became seriously isolated. The coast of the Red Sea was taken by the Arabs, and trade decreased. At the same time, attacks came from the pagan Agau peoples to the south.

From 700 to 1000, Aksum or Abyssinia, as it was now called, declined in wealth and power. These three centuries are called the 'dark ages' of Aksum. There were repeated invasions from the north and the east. In about 980, the king wrote to the ruler of Nubia, far away down the Nile. The country, he said, lay in ruins. He begged for help, but no help came.

The Zagwe kings

At last the tide turned. It happened in a strange way. The pagan Agau invaders from the south themselves became Christians. They then succeeded in overthrowing the Semitic line of kings, who were supposed to be descended from King Solomon of Israel. In its place, in 1137, they started a new line of kings called the Zagwe.

Under the rule of the Zagwe, two things happened. First, the Christian church revived. The number of hermits—religious men living alone—and monks—religious men living in communities called monasteries—increased. New churches were built where people could worship.

King Lalibela, indeed, ordered churches to be hewn out of the solid rock. Several churches were made in this way. A block of stone would be separated from the hill by digging a

This church at Lalibela was hewn out of the rock

A Christian saint of Ethiopia (rock-carving)

Zara Yakob

trench all round it. Inside, the rock was hollowed out, but leaving pillars and arches. The roof of the church reached to the original ground level. A legend grew up which said that angels used to come and continue the work at night while the builders were asleep. The most famous of these churches is at Roha, and it is still used today.

However, the Zagwe kings, being of the Agau tribe, brought new customs into the practice of the church in Ethiopia, so that it became even more different from other Christian churches than before.

The second change brought by the Zagwe kings was that the centre of the Abyssinian kingdom moved southward. It moved away from the country of Tigre around Aksum, south into the highlands of Amhara around Lake Tana. This was partly because the Zagwe themselves came from the south. It was also because the highlands of the south were more easily defended against the Moslem invaders. This rugged country, with its steep and jagged mountains, was always hard to conquer. It explains why the Ethiopians have kept their independence right down to the present day.

In spite of their successes, the Zagwe were not liked by the Semitic ruling class of Abyssinia. In 1270 there was a rebellion.

*The Kingdom of Abyssinia
1200 to 1530*

The last Zagwe king took refuge in a church, but he was caught and killed there. The old Solomonic line of kings was restored.

After these disturbances, Abyssinia continued to prosper for another two centuries. Under the great king Zara Yakob (1434–1468), the frontiers of Abyssinia were extended. The Moslem states were pushed back to the coastal plain. Within the country the power of the king was increased, and the church and the monarchy were closely united.

Then came disaster. The Moslems to the east, who had their capital at Harar, decided to take revenge on Abyssinia for previous defeats. Led by an energetic general, Ahmad the Left-handed, they swept across the plateau in 1529, burning churches and plundering monasteries. Much of Ethiopian civilization was destroyed.

**Abyssinia and the
Portuguese**

At this desperate time the king of Abyssinia, Lebna Dengel, remembered the visit of some Europeans a few years before. These had been Portuguese, who had arrived from the coast (see Chapter 9 of Book Two). They had announced that they were members of the Roman Catholic Church, and had invited the Christians of Abyssinia to join the Roman Church and become their allies. They had stayed six years in the country, but had met with no success. Now, attacked by Moslems, the king sent a message to Europe, saying that Abyssinia would join the Roman Church if the Portuguese would come to his aid.

Lebna died in 1540, but in reply to his call a Portuguese force of four hundred men led by Christopher da Gama arrived at Massawa in 1541. After some small-scale fighting, the Portuguese and the Abyssinians together met the Moslems near Lake Tana, and defeated them in a decisive battle. Ahmad the Left-handed was killed, and Abyssinia was saved.

Friendship with Portugal continued for some years afterwards. However, the next king decided not to join his church with the Church of Rome after all. In spite of the efforts of Jesuit missionaries, the Abyssinian Church remained independent. As we shall see, by 1700 the Portuguese were driven from the coast of East Africa by the Arabs.

And so, in spite of Moslem attacks, Portuguese influence and the great Galla migration (see Chapter 10 of Book Two), Ethiopia continued in its mountain stronghold, as an independent African state, with an independent African Christian Church, through all the centuries of African history which we read about in this book.

The power of the king in Ethiopia

When our king Zara Yakob went into the district of Axum to fulfil the law and the rite of coronation according to the rites followed by his ancestors, all of the inhabitants, as well as the priests, went to meet him and welcomed him with great rejoicing.

When he entered the gates of the town, the king had on his right hand and on his left the governor of Tigre and the administrator of Aksum who carried olive branches according to custom. After arriving within the walls, the king had brought to him much gold, which he scattered as far as the city gate on the carpets which were spread along his route.

During his stay at Aksum, our king regulated all the institutions of the Church and prescribed to be recited each day, at canonical hours, prayers which up to that time had been neglected.

The king placed at the head of each province one of his sisters, entrusted with administering the district in his name. Later the king himself took in hand the government of the whole of Ethiopia. All the people trembled before the undaunted might of the king.

from the *Chronicle of the Emperor*
Zara Yakob 1518

North-east African Time Chart

Date	Meroe	Ethiopia	East Coast
500 B.C. 400	Kushites move capital from Napata to Meroe. Knowledge of iron spreading to Meroe.	More Hamites from Arabia settling in Ethiopia.	Hindu traders from India begin to visit the East Coast of Africa. Phoenicians sail round Africa?
300	Great age of Meroe begins.		Indonesians settling in Madagascar and on east coast.
200			
100	Romans conquer Egypt. Queen of Meroe attacks Romans.	Growth of Aksum with port at Adulis as centre of trade between Upper Nile and Red Sea.	*Periplus of the Erythrean Sea* written by Greek trader.
A.D.	Punitive expedition to Napata.		
100	Decline of Meroe begins.		
200		Aksum now capital of great kingdom.	
300	Meroe destroyed by the Aksumites.	King Ezana destroys Meroe. First obelisks set up. Christianity accepted in Aksum. Great age of Aksum.	Rhapta and other 'Azanian' coastal towns flourishing on Arabian and Indian trade.
400			
500			
600		THE HIJRA 622	
700		Moslems conquer Egypt and Red Sea coast. 'Dark Age' of Aksum begins.	Arab and Persian settlements begin as far south as Kilwa.
800			Decline of Rhapta and other African coast towns. El Masoudi makes first report of black people living on the east coast.
900		Appeal from King of Aksum to King of Nubia goes unanswered.	
1000			Kilwa grows into a large town. Kilwa gains control of Sofala.
1100		Zagwe line of kings set up. Rock-hewn churches built. Centre of kingdom moves south to Amhara.	
1200		Last Zagwe King overthrown. Solomonic line restored.	'Golden Age' of Kilwa begins.
1300			
1400		Conquests of King Zara Yakob.	Kilwa begins to decline. Rise of Pate. Sofala becomes independent.
1500		New Moslem invasion. Appeal to Portuguese for help. Moslems driven out of Abyssinia. Isolation of Abyssinia continues.	Portuguese arrive on east coast. Kilwa and other towns captured. Fort Jesus built at Mombasa.
1600			Seif bin Sultan attacks Mombasa, takes Fort Jesus.
1700			Portuguese driven from east coast north of Mozambique.
1800			

12 Stone builders of the south-east

In Chapter 10 you read about the early Hamites in East Africa. They had arrived about A.D. 300, or perhaps before, and lived side by side with the Bushmen of old. In the south-west they even mixed with the Bushmen, and formed the Hottentot people.

After them came some of the first Bantu-speaking tribes, such as the Tonga. The Tonga settled down in the Zambezi valley between A.D. 500 and 1000. Others, such as the Makwa, went to live in the coast country between Lake Malawi and the sea.

Following these early tribes, others came, slowly making their way south. Among them were peoples whom we call southern Bantu. These were the Nguni and the Sotho peoples, who now live in South Africa and Botswana. They brought cattle with them, and moved on year after year, looking for the best grazing grounds. You will read more about them in Chapter 12 of Book Two.

The early Shona

Some time before A.D. 1000 there came to Zambezi country an early Shona tribe called Karanga.

When and where did the Karanga become a tribe? This is something we cannot tell, for of course they kept no written records. But the stories told by their old men today say that they came from the land east of Lake Tanganyika. Some people even think that 'Tanganyika' is really a Shona word.

Now we believe that Persians and Arabs were trading on the east coast by A.D. 900, and that by that time some early Swahili words were being used by inland tribes. But the Shona have no early Swahili words in their language, so we think that they probably left Tanganyika before 900.

Before they came to Tanganyika, of course, the Shona had come from even farther north. Perhaps for a long time they had lived north of Lake Nyanza, and had even mixed with Hamites from Ethiopia.

After moving slowly from place to place, perhaps making villages in the Muchinga Highlands west of the Luangwa River, the Karanga came to the Zambezi. A Shona headman, speaking about fifty years ago, said that they crossed the river near Urungwe Mountain, which is not far from Chirundu. There they found the Tavara and the Valley Tonga.

Karanga kingdom of Guruuswa

Beyond the valley was hilly country, so the Karanga moved on, looking for good pasture. At last they found the grassy plains of present-day Mashonaland and Matabeleland, which they called Guruuswa. There was more rain then than there is today, and even towards the Kalahari the grass was good.

Here lived the Bushmen, whom the Karanga called *Mandionerepi*, which means 'How did you catch a glimpse of me?', because they were quick runners and always darted out of sight. Here also lived a few brown-skinned Hamitic people, from far-off Ethiopia long ago. Some early Sotho also had their villages in the south.

The Karanga drove out the Bushmen, because these Stone Age hunters kept killing their cattle. They conquered the Hamites and made them herd cattle for them. The early Sotho fled across the Limpopo to the country which today we call the Transvaal.

By about 1100 the Karanga controlled all the country between the Zambezi and the Limpopo. Now they settled down. They built villages of round huts with strongly built walls of pole and mud called *daga*. They made new kinds of clay pots, some with long, high necks. Graphite was rubbed on the side of the pot to make it shine. They mined iron for making arrowheads, spears and axes.

The Karanga also found gold in the ground. Perhaps the people who lived there before them showed them where the gold was. At first the Karanga were not very interested. Gold was too soft for most uses. They made it into beads for women, especially those in the royal family. Before long, however, when Arab traders came to the country, they mined for gold a great deal more, because with it they could buy cloth and other goods.

Zimbabwe

The Karanga made their first capital in the south. Here they found a valley where the grass was green most of the year, because of mists that blew up from the Sabi valley and from the sea.

(Right) Part of the remains of Zimbabwe

In the middle of the valley was a high rock which they called Mwanha Hill. At one end of the rock was a flat space where huts were built. Soon, however, stone walls were built to make the rock safer from attack. The stones were made from the granite blocks that lay about on the ground. Granite is a kind of rock which splits easily into square shapes. The Karanga had not built in stone before. Their first stone walls were roughly made, but as time went on they became better builders. The walls they built are still standing there today.

Mwanha Hill came to be called *Zimbabwe* which means 'a place of stone'. It was used for defence in time of war. Also, because it was so safe, it was used for a shrine, or place of worship. The Karanga believed in a god whom they called Mwari, who was the creator of all men.

There is much granite in Mashonaland and Matabeleland, so the Karanga built stone forts in many other places. These 'little zimbabwes' were smaller than the fort at Mwanha Hill. Sometimes they were used for defence, sometimes, perhaps, for cattle kraals. The best-known ones, which you can still see, although they are in ruins now, were at Khami and Dhlo Dhlo.

However, the people did not like to live in stone houses. Their huts were still made of pole and daga, with thatched roofs, as they had always been.

The big fort at Mwanha Hill became so famous that news of it reached the Arabs at Sofala far away on the coast. One day, perhaps about 1100, some Arab traders travelled up the Sabi valley and reached the Karanga capital. They marvelled at the stone walls, and even more at the gold and ivory used by the people. They took some gold dust and ivory, and in exchange gave cloth and glass beads. The Karanga wanted the glass beads, for they had bright colours which they did not know how to make. Soon the Arabs were coming every year to trade.

Mutota, the first Monomotapa

Some time about 1400, the Karanga began to grow restless. Their numbers had increased. Their cattle were so many that there was not enough grazing. Above all, salt was hard to find.

The king decided to send out an expedition to look for better land. After some weeks, the party came back with news of good salt supplies towards the Zambezi River, which the Karanga called the Dande. The leader even brought a block of salt to prove it.

The king's eldest son, Mutota, was a good hunter and a brave warrior, and he longed to lead an army to win new lands for his people. The old king gave his consent, and preparations were made amid rejoicing and festivities at the capital. When all was nearly ready, the old king died, and Mutota was accepted in his place. Saddened by this event, Mutota none the less decided to go forward, and marched north with a large army.

The Tavara in the Zambezi valley were amazed at the numbers of the Karanga. They compared them to locusts, which sometimes invaded the country in clouds. Ever since, the Shona in that part have been called *Makorekore*, which is the Karanga word for 'locusts'.

Mutota conquered the Tavara easily, drove away herds of their cattle, and carried away loads of their grain. The Tavara called Mutota *Mwene Mutapa*, which means 'master plunderer'. This name has also lived on as *Monomotapa*, which is how the Portuguese spelt it. It became the title of Mutota and of his successors.

The Empire of Monomotapa

Mutota built his new capital at Fura Mountain beside the Utete River, in northern Mashonaland. Different clans were settled in different parts of the kingdom, and Mutota appointed each of his sons as governor of a province. More gold was found in this part of the country, and Arabs came up from the Zambezi to trade.

By 1450, Mutota was growing old. His sons were behaving badly towards him. They traded separately with the Arabs, and showed him no respect. Just before he died, therefore, Mutota named his daughter Nyamhita to be his heir.

Baobab tree

Now Mutota's chief wife revealed a secret command which the king had made, that the son who married Nyamhita would become the chief. In Karanga custom, the wives of the dead king had great power in choosing the successor. But of all the twelve sons, only the youngest, Matope, would agree to this. So Matope married Nyamhita, his half-sister, and they became king and queen. Mutota's body was buried in a cave near his hut, and eight baobab trees were planted round the site of his village. Two of them are still standing today.

Matope ruled from 1450 to 1480. He strengthened the Karanga army, and made his empire greater than it had been in his father's time. He even raided Malawi country across the Zambezi as far as Karonga's village on the Nyasa-Tanganyika plateau. Trade increased, and many Arabs came to live in Mashonaland.

Two kingdoms

Matope had many children. One of them was his son by a wife of lowly status, and so was given the name *Changa*, which means 'the unimportant one'.

Changa, however, grew up to be a man of great energy and strength of will. When he reached manhood, he was made the governor of the Rozwi province in the south. The Rozwi were a Karanga clan who lived in the country around Great Zimbabwe, the first Karanga capital. They were now becoming a powerful tribe.

Changa came to be regarded as the chief of the Rozwi tribe. The Arabs who came to Zimbabwe were impressed with his power. They gave him the title of *Amir*, which in Arabic means a powerful lord. For this reason Changa, and his sons who were chiefs after him, were known by the title of *Changamire*.

Changamire I even attacked northern Mashonaland, but although he killed Monomotapa Nyahuma, he was driven out by Nyahuma's son, and after that remained in the south. Thus there were now two strong kingdoms in Mashonaland—Monomotapa's Karanga empire in the north, and Changamire's Rozwi kingdom in the south. This situation continued for the next two hundred years.

The temple at Zimbabwe

These two centuries from 1500 to 1700 were very important in the history of Mashonaland, for three reasons.

First, it was the time when the Great Zimbabwe temple was built at Changamire's capital. All this time, work had been

The temple at Zimbabwe. The round tower is among the trees on the right

Ground plan of the temple: A, North entrance; B, North-west entrance; C, West entrance; D, Great Wall; E, Entrance to parallel passage; F, Round tower

continuing on the walls of the defence fort at Mwanha Hill. Under Changamire I, these walls were now completed, and a line of stone pillars topped the great western rampart.

Next the Rozwi started to build a huge stone enclosure on the flat ground a quarter of a mile to the south-east. This enclosure was a hundred yards long and seventy yards wide, and oval or rounded in shape. The walls were thirty feet thick in some parts and, when finished, thirty-two feet tall at the highest place. Inside were smaller stone enclosures, long passage walls and a high round stone tower. By this time the Rozwi had become clever stone builders, and the stones on the outside of the walls were carefully shaped, and fitted together exactly without cement. Many thousands of well-shaped stones were quarried to make this building. We do not know how long it took to complete. Perhaps it was over a hundred years. Certainly by 1700 the temple was finished.

We call this building a temple because it is believed that the Rozwi used it as a shrine to the god Mwari. Perhaps it was used as a kraal or paddock for the sacred bulls of the tribe. The old shrine on Mwanha Hill would have been too small for this purpose.

Divine kingship

The second great development during these two centuries was the growth of a new strong kingship. About 1500, Monomotapa and Changamire were the two strongest kings in Southern Africa.

The power of the king was partly based on religious belief. The Karanga, as we have seen, believed in a Creator or God who was called Mwari. This was quite an advanced belief, because many African tribes, in the way of primitive peoples, believed in many gods. The Karanga believed in one god. Mwari controlled the life of the people. If the crops failed, or other trouble came, the spirits of the dead ancestors of the tribe, called *mhondoro*, must speak with Mwari. But only the king, and no other person, could speak with the *mhondoro*. So among the Karanga the king was high priest as well as ruler. Monomotapa was a kind of priest-king. Perhaps this idea had come long ago from Egypt far to the north.

Monomotapa lived in great state. He did not build in stone, because the rocks were not so good in northern Mashonaland. His palace, a large building of pole and daga with a thatched roof, had a great fence round it. He was surrounded by his wives and many attendants. He carried three finely made sticks or wands, and if a certain man was to die Monomotapa would let fall one of these wands. This was the signal for execution. No man could look on Monomotapa while speaking to him. It was the rule for the visitor to lie on the ground, turning away his face and slowly clapping his hands together.

It was also the rule that Monomotapa had to be perfect in health. If he became ill, or was injured, he had to take poison. Later, however, this practice was stopped. Before he died, the king used to name one of his sons to succeed him. Messengers would travel throughout the kingdom announcing the new chief.

Trade

The third important happening was the growth of trade.

We have seen how the Arabs came to Zimbabwe town as early as 1100. They came for ivory and gold, and brought glass beads and cloth and other goods.

After 1400 many more Arabs came, and by 1500 perhaps ten thousand of them were living in Mashonaland. They were not interested in bringing education and the Moslem faith to the Karanga, as the Berbers were doing at this time among the peoples of the Niger. Their only object was trade. Every year,

*Copper gong
from Zimbabwe*

Arabs came up the long trail from Sofala, and visited Zimbabwe and Fura Mountain and many other places. More cotton came into the country. The rich people among the Rozwi and the Karanga wore cotton robes.

The wealth which this trade brought them enabled the Rozwi to build the Zimbabwe temple. Gold mining increased, and the Arabs took much gold from the country. They also took copper and ivory, but they did not take slaves. Monomotapa and other Shona chiefs were able to refuse to sell slaves, because their armies were strong, and even more because they had gold to sell instead.

The Karanga also traded with the Luba people in the north. The Luba lived among the Congo tributaries. You will read about them in Chapter 7 of Book Two. Their country of Katanga was rich in copper, and they used to make H-shaped copper ingots for trade, and also copper ornaments and gongs. These gongs were used on ceremonial occasions at the royal court. Ingots and gongs from Katanga have been found at Great Zimbabwe.

Lastly, the Karanga traded with the Portuguese. The Portuguese came to Mashonaland, because they had heard from the Arabs about the gold. Because of quarrels between the Portuguese and the Arabs, and between the Portuguese and the Karanga, the Empire of Monomotapa began to break up, and trade decreased. Changamire in the south came to be the strongest ruler in the country.

Rozwi conquest

In 1693 Monomotapa again quarrelled with the Portuguese. He asked Changamire to help him drive them away. Changa marched north with an army of several thousand spearmen. However, he not only killed or drove out all the Portuguese. He went on to attack Monomotapa, and defeated him. Now Changamire was *Mambo* or king of all Mashonaland.

But the war had damaged trade. Few Arabs were now in the country, and no Europeans. Although the Rozwi kings ruled for more than a hundred years, they were no longer so wealthy. They did not make any more stone buildings, and mining for gold declined. The organized society which the Karanga had begun to form stopped developing. There were several reasons for this: one was geographical. Mashonaland is on a plateau far from the sea, and waterfalls made it impossible to sail boats there. The coastal plain was unhealthy for travellers. More-over, the country is very far from Europe and Arabia, from which new ideas could come. Books and writing never spread among the Karanga. Finally, the Portuguese and Arabs, who could have brought new knowledge, fought against each other and were in the end driven from the country.

In 1830 the Rozwi were attacked by the Ngoni, a warrior tribe from the south. You will read about this in Chapter 12 of Book Two. The Ngoni killed many Rozwi and burned their villages. It was the end of the Rozwi kingdom in Mashonaland.

Monomotapa's Empire

Of the mines of this land from which the gold is taken, the nearest to Sofala are those which they call Manica, which are in a plain surrounded by mountains having a circumference of about thirty leagues.

There are other mines in a district called Toroa, ruled by a vassal of Monomotapa, and these mines are the most ancient known in the country. They are all in the plain, in the midst of which is a fortress, of masonry within and without, built of stones of marvellous size, and there appears to be no mortar joining them. The wall is more than twenty-five spans in width, and the height is not so great considering the width.

The natives of the country call all these edifices Symbaoe (Zimbabwe), which in their language signifies 'court', for every place where Monomotapa may be is so called.

Joao de Barros, about 1550

In the whole kingdom of Vealanga (Vakaranga), gold is extracted; and in this way: they dig out the earth and make a kind of tunnel, through which they go under the ground a long stone's throw, and keep on taking out from the veins with the ground mixed with the gold, and, when collected, they put it in a pot, and cook it in much fire; and after cooking they take it out, and put it to cool, and, when cold, the earth remains, and the gold all fine gold. . . . And no man can take it out without leave from the king, under penalty of death.

Diogo de Alcancova, about 1506

If the Cafars have a suit, and seek to speak with the King, they creep to the place where he is, having prostrated themselves at the entrance, and look not on him all the while they speak, but lying on one side clap their hands all the time; and then having finished,

Bird, carved in soapstone, from Zimbabwe

they creep out of the doors as they came in. For no Cafar may enter on foot to speak to the King, nor eye him when speaking, except the particular friends of the King.

The Portugals enter on their feet, but unshod, and being near the King, prostrate themselves lying on one side almost sitting, and without looking on him speak to him, at every fourth word clapping their hands according to the custom.

Both Cafars and Portugals are entertained by him with wine of maize, or their wheat, called Pombe, which they must drink, although against stomach, not to contemn the King's bountie; whence the Portugals have had some trouble, and are forced to stay in town without leave to return home. . . . .

Joao dos Santos, about 1550

13 Early trade in the Indian Ocean

When the Arabs came to the Rozwi capital in about 1150, they had walked all the way from the sea coast. Even then the coast from which they had come was not their home. They had come to that part of the coast from Kilwa, perhaps from Mogadishu, or even from Arabia far to the north.

Nor were the Arabs the first people to sail their boats down the shore of East Africa. Men had been sailing on the Indian Ocean for over two thousand years. Their purpose was trade. Let us go back to the beginning, and read about this trade.

Civilization in the Far East

You will remember that farming, building and writing began in the valley of the Nile, about 3000 B.C. You will remember also that similar developments took place in the Euphrates valley. These early beginnings formed the civilizations of Egypt and Sumer.

The same sort of beginnings happened in two other places, much farther east. The first place was along the River Indus, between Persia and North India. From here Indian boats began to sail along the coasts of India and Arabia after 2000 B.C.

The other place was much farther away still, in the valley of the Hwang Ho River in China. Here, too, people began farming and trading, even before the days of early Egypt. The Hwang Ho people became great sailors and traders. At first small boats sailed in the Yellow Sea. Then sailors in bigger boats traded in the islands of the East Indies. They went to Malaya and Java. Once or twice, Chinese travellers went even as far as India.

So by 1000 B.C. there were Chinese, Indonesian, Indian, Persian and Arab ships sailing on the coasts of the Indian Ocean. After a time, a few Phoenician and Egyptian ships appeared as well.

The monsoon

All these ships used to keep close to the land. The sailors were afraid of storms, and liked to be able to come quickly to the shore.

Sailors in the Arabian sea, however, found that the wind always blows steadily from India to Africa during the northern winter from October to March. During the northern summer,

Sea trade between China, India and Africa about 1000 B.C.

CHINA

INDIA

AFRICA

'Azania'

Winter monsoon

Summer monsoon

INDIAN OCEAN

INDONESIA

MADAGASCAR

0°

0°

Traders
⟹ Indonesian
➤ Indian
⟹ Chinese
⟹ Arab and Persian

0   1000   2000   3000
Miles

Notice how the traders sailed close to the land

from April to September, the wind blows in the opposite direction. Gaining confidence, they allowed this wind, which we call the *monsoon*, to take them across the Arabian Sea to Africa. From the inhabitants, who were probably early Hamites from the north-east, the sailors found that they could obtain ivory.

After waiting for some months the sailors found that the wind, as they expected, changed direction and blew again from the south-west. They sailed back to the Persian Gulf, or to India, from which they had come.

As time went on, more and more traders came to the east coast of Africa in this way.

Traders from the Far East

Sometimes traders came from Indonesia, Malaya, Polynesia and even China to buy from Indian traders. From China they brought glass beads and porcelain plates and vases, and different kinds of cloth. A few of these eastern goods were then brought by Indians and Arabians to the African coast, where they could be exchanged for ivory. This trade from India and the Far East was beginning to reach East Africa about 600 B.C.

Sometimes traders used to build houses on the African coast and stay there. Thus, when the population of Indonesia began to increase when the use of iron was discovered there soon after the beginning of our era, it was natural for settlers to come to East Africa to find new homes.

The arrival of these settlers from Indonesia was especially important for Africa, because they brought with them new crops. The most successful was the Asian banana, which was of a better type than any growing in Africa at that time. This new plant spread rapidly through tropical Africa just when the Iron Age tribes were migrating southward, and it helped to support the new population.

Indonesians came in largest numbers to the island of Madagascar. They were the main ancestors of the Malagasy people of today. Some of them also settled on the South African coast, and later were absorbed by the southern Bantu who began to arrive about A.D. 1000.

However, these people from the east were not the only foreign visitors to Africa's coasts.

Sailors from the Mediterranean

We read in an earlier chapter how by 600 B.C. there were many sailors trading in the Mediterranean Sea. There were the Egyptians and the Greeks and, most important, the Phoenicians.

It was of course impossible for boats in the Mediterranean to sail to the Indian Ocean, because of the strip of land at Sinai which joins Africa to Asia. Ships were, however, sometimes built on the Red Sea, and you will remember the story of Queen Hatshepsut's expedition to Punt (see p. 41).

Usually these expeditions did not sail very far. About 500 B.C., however, Necho, Pharaoh of Egypt, sent a ship with Phoenician sailors to sail round Africa from the Red Sea to the Straits of Gibraltar. Of course he did not know how big Africa was: he thought it finished just south of Egypt, and he expected the sailors would soon come home. The Phoenicians, however, sailed on for month after month and then for another year, and yet another. They stopped each year to camp on the shore and plant crops to use for supplies in next season. At home King Necho thought they must all be dead. The Egyptians were surprised when the sailors arrived back after travelling for over three years, and reported that the sun had been on their right hand as they rounded the southern cape. They had, in fact, sailed right round Africa and returned to the Mediterranean through the Straits of Gibraltar. This story was written down by a Greek called Herodotus in 450 B.C.

The *Periplus* guide book

In the time of the Roman Empire, there was more trade and travel both by land and sea.

About the year A.D. 100 a Greek sailor wrote a guide book for eastern traders. It was called *The Periplus of the Erythrean Sea*, this being the Greek name for the Indian Ocean. It told about many countries, and how to go to them, as far as the land of T'sin, which was China. In particular, there were some pages telling about the east coast of Africa.

In the book this coast was called *Azania*. There were many islands off the coast, and in the islands there were many birds, tortoises and large lizards. There were also people living on the coast. The writer did not say that they were black, and we suppose that they were brown-skinned early Hamites. They used to catch fish in the sea channels by using reed baskets. They also fished from boats. These boats were made from rough planks, sewn together with fibre, and the writer called them 'sewn boats'. He was surprised to see them, because Greek and Roman boats were always made with nails. He called the last town on the coast *Rhapta*, from a Greek word meaning 'sewn'. The people of Rhapta and other towns, he said, were subjects of a chief in South Arabia. The site of Rhapta has disappeared with time (see Chapter 14), but probably it was near present-day Tanga.

Traders, according to the writer of the *Periplus*, could buy ivory and tortoise-shell, and oil from coconut palms. In exchange, they sold spear-heads and axes. The early Hamites of East Africa did not know about iron, and were pleased to be able to buy iron articles from Arabia.

Ptolemy's map of Africa

Fifty years later an educated Greek called Ptolemy read the *Periplus*, and found out all he could about Africa. Then he wrote it down in a geography book about the world as it was known at that time. In his book he drew a map of Africa, which shows what people in the Roman Empire thought Africa looked like.

Ptolemy did not, of course, know about the interior of Africa,

A copy of Ptolemy's map of the world. Much of it was guesswork

but there were rumours of mountains and lakes, so he made a good guess and drew what he thought. The result was interesting, as you can see. It was the last attempt to draw a map of Africa until the Italians and Portuguese became interested a thousand years later.

Bantu reported on the east coast

When the Roman Empire was destroyed after about A.D. 500, trade from the Mediterranean began to decrease and at last it stopped. Soon after this, when was no trade from Europe and no one to write about it, early Bantu groups began to reach the east coast from the great lakes. Some of them turned north and moved towards Somaliland. Others turned south and crossed the Rufiji River. We shall read more about these and later movements in Chapter 10 of Book Two.

We know of the arrival of the Bantu from Arab records. Arabs at this time were better educated than Europeans, and had some great travellers and geographers. One of these was Al Masoudi, who came to the east coast in 915. He was the first man to report seeing black-skinned people living on or near the coast.

The Arab word for 'black' was *zanj*. From this time onward the Arabs called East Africa 'the land of the Zanj', or *Zanj-el-Bar*.

A Chinese trader's description of East Africa

The land of Po-Pa-Li is in the South-Western Ocean. The people do not eat any cereals, but they eat meat. More frequently even, they prick a vein of one of their oxen, mix the blood with milk, and eat it raw. They have no clothes, but they wrap round their waists a sheep's skin, which hangs down and covers them. Their women are clean and well-behaved. The people of the country themselves kidnap them, and sell them to strangers at prices many times more than they would fetch at home. The products of the country are ivory and ambergris.*

When Persian traders wish to enter the country, they form a caravan of several thousand men, and present them with strips of cloth. All, whether old or young, draw blood and swear to an oath, and only then do they trade their goods.

From of old, this country has not been subject to any foreign power. In fighting, they use elephants' tusks, ribs and wild cattle's horns as spears, and they have corselets† and bows and arrows. The Arabs are continually making raids on them.

Tuan Ch'eng-Shih, c. 860

* A substance which comes from a whale. It is used for making perfume.
† A kind of body-armour made of leather.

14 Cities of the east coast

Trade with East Africa had been going on for hundreds of years. The traders did not, however, stay on the coast for more than a few months at a time. The towns on the coast, like Rhapta, were African towns and villages.

From about A.D. 650 this began to change. Arab and Persian settlers came to live in Africa. The Arabs were nomadic people living in the dry, sandy country of Arabia. They were Semitic, but were closely related to the Hamites who, by this time, had mostly been driven out of Arabia. Arabs living on the coast of Arabia had learned to sail and trade from the Persians. They sailed in strong wooden boats called *dhows*, which have one mast and a large sail. Important Arab trading towns were Muza on the Red Sea, and Muscat near the Persian Gulf.

When the Arabs and Persians came to live on the East African coast, they built new towns and gave them new names. Africans came to live and work in these towns. That is why the old towns like Rhapta have disappeared.

Settlers on the east coast

The first Arab arrivals came in about 660. This was soon after the religion of Islam, which we shall read about in Chapter 1 of Book Two, had been founded by Mohammed. There was a civil war in Arabia, during which some Arabs escaped by sailing away to the East African coast, probably landing near Mogadishu.

Here and farther south they found a hospitable, green palm-lined coast, a welcome change from the dry sands of Arabia. They sent news home, and as time went on other settlers came to join them and to make new colonies along the coast.

Soon Persians were joining the Arabs. An old story tells of Hasan bin Ali, the son of the Sultan of Shiraz on the Persian Gulf. Leaving home because of a quarrel, he sailed away to Africa with his six sons. These sons, according to the story, settled at different places on the coast, including Mombasa and Zanzibar. Hasan sailed on to the island of Kilwa.

On the island lived an Arab trader, a Moslem called Muriri wa Bari. Muriri told Hasan that the island was owned by an African, who was away hunting. When the owner returned, Hasan asked if he might buy the island. The African replied that he would sell it for as much cloth as would go right round the shore. Hasan agreed, and bought the island, which became known as Kilwa Kisiwani. In order to make it safe from attack, Hasan deepened the channel between the island and the mainland, so that no one could cross without a boat.

This story is a legend which probably has some truth. It shows two things. Firstly, Arab and Persian settlers often bought their land from the Africans for cloth, and probably other goods as well. Secondly, they liked to settle on islands away from the shore, to be secure from African attacks.

Within a few years, Kilwa grew to be an important town. In 1020 it was attacked by the people of Mafia, to the north, and the ruler, who was called the Sultan, fled to Zanzibar Island. After returning from Zanzibar with reinforcements, however, the Sultan conquered Mafia, and from that time Kilwa increased in wealth and importance.

Other settlements

There were many other Arab settlements. Though they never joined together under one government, there was usually a friendly agreement between them. Sometimes one town grew more powerful than the others; then it would try to control the trade from Sofala. Sofala was south of Kilwa and Mozambique, and was the port for the gold trade in Mashonaland. After about A.D. 1000 the Arabs often used to go there. The town which controlled Sofala could be wealthy and strong.

At first, Mogadishu took the Sofala gold. There were more Arabs living at Mogadishu because it was farthest north and nearest Arabia.

South of Mogadishu were Pate, Lamu, Malindi, Gedi, Mombasa, Pemba, Zanzibar and Kilwa. You can see these on the map. Zanzibar was still only a village, and did not become an important place till later on.

About 1130, the Sultan of Kilwa sent settlers to Sofala and took control of the gold trade. Kilwa was nearest to Sofala, so this was easy for the Sultan to do. Now Kilwa became the most powerful town on the coast, and very wealthy. A mosque and a palace and many stone houses were built. The 'golden age of Kilwa' lasted from 1200 to 1400.

After that, Pate was trading with Sofala and became a rival of Kilwa. Sofala became an independent town.

Swahili people

The rulers of the coast towns were called Sultans. There was a Sultan of Kilwa, a Sultan of Mombasa, and a Sultan of Malindi. The Sultan was usually an Arab, except for the Sultan of Malindi, who was a Persian. The Wazir and the Amir, the two chief ministers of the Sultan, were usually Arabs too. Many of the rich merchants and owners of plantations were Arabs.

However, most of the people were Bantu. Now many of the Arabs took Bantu wives, and the children of these marriages began to form a new people. They came to be called Swahili. Children learn the language their mothers speak, so that the Swahili language is very like the Bantu tongue.

After a time there were a number of wealthy and powerful Swahili living in the coast towns, though most Swahili remained poor and had to work very hard.

Life of the people

The poorer people in towns like Kilwa, Mombasa and Gedi lived in wooden houses with roofs of grass or palm leaves. Even more important people had wooden houses at first. Later, when some merchants became rich, they built houses of stone. The stone they used was the rough coral that lies along the shore and underneath the sea.

Ruins of the palace at Gedi

The Sultan's palace was built of stone; so was the mosque,

where people worshipped Allah, the one true God. Some of these mosques were destroyed by the Portuguese later, when there was fighting, because the Portuguese were Christians and thought the Moslems were wrong. The ruins of these mosques can still be seen.

The mosque at Kilwa had many pillars. The roof above the pillars was of round domes, called cupolas, looking like pots turned upside down. This was how people built mosques in Arabia. It helped to make the mosque cool inside, so that people could pray quietly.

Inside the palace of the Sultan and the houses of rich merchants, people liked to have Persian rugs on the floor and hanging on the wall. Also on the wall they hung porcelain dishes from China.

Exports

The rugs from Persia and the dishes from China were paid for by African goods. The most important of the exports from Africa was ivory.

People in China could find most of the things they wanted in their own country, but there were no elephants and no ivory. Yet they loved ivory. They made it into all kinds of beautiful things such as chessmen, figures, knife handles, buttons, bracelets and combs.

The Chinese had found out about African ivory from Indian traders. In A.D. 860 a Chinese sailor called Tuan went to see for himself. He reached Somaliland, and described the Hamitic pastoralists who lived there. 'The products of the country', wrote Tuan, 'are ivory and ambergris.'

Cowrie shell

None the less it was rare for the Chinese to send ships to Africa, because it was too far away. Mostly they bought ivory from Arab and Indian ships, which carried it as far as the East Indies.

Sometimes wild animals were taken in ships. In 1415 the Emperor of China was presented with a giraffe from East Africa. There is a painting of this giraffe in the museum in Peking. Tortoise-shell, rhinoceros horn and leopard skins, which people in India and China thought were very valuable, were also traded by the Arabs. Lastly, there was gold.

Some of the African gold came from Ethiopia, but most of it came from Sofala. The Arabs went every year to see the Shona chiefs. Gold from Mashonaland went all over the world.

Chinese porcelain bowl from Gedi

Coins

Kilwa coin (both sides)

Arabs and the interior

In exchange for the gold and ivory and other things, the Arabs liked to buy porcelain and cloth. Chinese porcelain was harder than Persian ware, and it did not break so easily. The blue and white colour was attractive to look at.

The Arabs used the cloth for making into clothes for their own people in the towns. They also sold it to the inland tribes. Cotton does not grow easily in Africa, and the Bantu did not know about it. Their own clothes were made of skin and bark cloth. They liked the bright cotton cloth from the east and paid a lot of gold and ivory for it.

After a long time, the traders wanted to use money instead of just exchanging goods. At first they collected rare sea shells, called cowries, from the shore. These became valuable, and one cowrie shell would pay for a length of cloth.

However, the Sultans wanted to be able to make their own money when they needed it. They knew that, in Europe, people had used metal coins since Roman times. One or two of the richer Sultans decided to make their own coins. Mogadishu and Kilwa had their own. They were made of copper.

Here is a picture of a coin made by Suleiman bin Hasan, ruler of Kilwa in about 1310. The writing on the front says: 'Suleiman, son of Al-Hasan, may he be happy!' On the back it says: 'Trust in the master of bounties. He is glorious!'

The Arabs did not try to live inland. They stayed by the coast. Travel inland was difficult and dangerous. They were not empire-builders, but traders, and they liked the sea.

South-Central African Time Chart

Date	Southern Africa	Mashonaland	East coast
A.D.	Sparsely inhabited by Stone Age Bushmen and Hottentots.	Inhabited by Bushmen, with some early Hamites, all of Stone Age culture.	Some Indian traders had long been visiting the east coast.
100			*Periplus of Erythrean Sea* written by Greek trader.
200			
300			Rhapta and other 'Azanian' coastal towns flourishing on Arabian and Indian trade.
400			
500			
600		Early Iron Age Bantu settlers probably arriving.	Arab and Persian settlements begin as far south as Kilwa.
700			Decline of Rhapta and other African coast towns.
800		Early Karanga (Shona) moving south from Lake Tanganyika.	
900	First southern Bantu move south of the Limpopo at about this time.		El Masoudi makes first report of black people living on the east coast.
1000	Early Sotho and Nguni groups cross Limpopo southward.	Karanga cross the Zambezi. Karanga kingdom set up between Zambezi and Limpopo. 'Acropolis' building begun at Great Zimbabwe. Arabs visit Mashonaland. Trade begins with Sofala.	Kilwa grows into a large town.
1100			Kilwa gains control of Sofala.
1200			'Golden Age' of Kilwa begins.
1300	Sotho and Nguni slowly move southward, driving out Bushmen.		
1400		Mutota becomes first Monomotapa. Rozwi split away under Changa. Great temple begun at Zimbabwe. Acropolis completed. Portuguese come to Mashonaland. Silveira martyred.	Kilwa begins to decline. Rise of Pate. Sofala becomes independent. Portuguese arrive on east coast. Kilwa and other towns captured.
1500			Fort Jesus built at Mombasa.
1600	Sotho established in Botswana and along the Orange River.	Zimba raids. Arab influence returns. Monomatapa drives out Portuguese with Rozwi aid. Rozwi empire established. Great temple completed.	Zimba raiders destroyed. Seif bin Sultan attacks Mombasa, takes Fort Jesus. Portuguese driven from east coast north of Mozambique.
1700	Nguni in Natal, now meeting Dutch settlers from the Cape.		

Questions and exercises

These questions are included for general guidance. Teachers will of course have other exercises and questions of their own. In particular, pupils should be encouraged to illustrate their notebooks with maps and drawings taken from the text.

Chapter 1

1 Find out as much as you can about what happened in your nearest town or village a year ago. Write a report. What methods will you use?

2 What is 'pre-literate history'? Write down four different ways in which this kind of history can be discovered.

Chapter 2

1 How were the first early men different from the early apes? Write down all the differences you can find in this chapter.

2 Write down all the ways you can think of in which fire proved useful to early man. Was it ever dangerous?

3 How did climate help in the development of early man?

Chapter 3

1 Make a copy of the Bushman drawing on p. 99. Explain why Late Stone Age men began to paint pictures.

2 Write all you can about hunting in the Late Stone Age.

3 'He was man the worker, man the artist and man the worshipper' (see p. 31). Explain this statement.

Chapter 4

1 What difference did agriculture and herding make in the life of Late Stone Age men?

2 Why were the Nile floods so important to the early Nile valley people?

Chapter 5	1 How did trade begin in the Nile valley?
	2 Imagine that you are an engineer employed in building one of the great pyramids. Write all you can about your work.
	3 Copy some hieroglyphic symbols into your notebook. What does 'hieroglyphic' mean?
Chapter 6	1 Describe the advantages of (*a*) copper and (*b*) bronze over stone in the making of buildings, tools and weapons.
	2 Explain how and why the Egyptian Empire and civilization came to an end.
Chapter 7	1 Write down three things which the Greeks contributed to civilization. Write a few lines on each.
	2 Make a copy of the map of the Roman Empire.
	3 What influence did the Romans have on North Africa?
Chapter 8	1 Explain why a prosperous kingdom grew up at Meroe after 300 B.C.
	2 Describe three important ways in which Meroe influenced the rest of Africa.
	3 Explain why the kingdom of Meroe declined and finally disappeared.
Chapter 9	1 Give three reasons why the civilizations of the Mediterranean did not spread into tropical Africa.
	2 Write all you can about the origin of the Negroes.
	3 Draw a map of the Sahara trade routes.
Chapter 10	1 Make a list of the Hamitic customs mentioned in this chapter. Why were the Hamites so called?
	2 What parts of Africa did the early Hamites settle in?

3 Why are the Bantu peoples called by this name? Where did they come from? Draw a map to show their migration through Africa.

Chapter 11   1 Tell the story of how Christianity came to Aksum.

2 What was achieved by the Zagwe kings?

3 Explain why Ethiopia was isolated for so long.

Chapter 12   1 Write all you can about Mutota, the first Monomotapa.

2 Draw the plan of the Great Zimbabwe and explain how it came to be built.

3 Describe the trade of Monomotapa's empire.

Chapter 13   1 Explain how the monsoon winds helped the traders in the Indian Ocean.

2 Make a list of the different traders along the East Coast mentioned in this chapter, and write a few sentences about each.

3 What can we learn from the author of the *Periplus* about the inhabitants of East Africa in A.D. 100?

Chapter 14   1 Why did the Arabs first come to settle on the east coast of Africa?

2 Write all you can about East African trade during the great age of Kilwa.

3 Draw a map of the east coast and mark in the Arab towns.

Index

THE STORY OF AFRICA
from the earliest times

Book Two

A. J. Wills

AFRICANA PUBLISHING CORPORATION
NEW YORK

Preface

The aim of this two-year course, of which this volume is the second part, is to provide an overall history of Africa for junior secondary schools. The continent and its peoples are treated as a whole, and their story is set in the perspective of world developments since ancient and classical times. It is hoped that such a course will provide the basis of a more detailed regional study later. In learning about the origin and history of peoples in other regions of the continent, African children can gain a better understanding of how their own background fits into the whole.

The first book, after describing the origins of man in Africa, the influence of the early civilizations, and the great migrations of the Iron Age, concluded with the early medieval history of East Africa, both inland and on the coast.

This second-year book deals first with Islam in North Africa, and then with the West African empires and the forest kingdoms, including the medieval period. An account of the arrival of Portuguese and other traders from overseas both on the west and the east coasts is followed by chapters on the interior of east and south-east Africa from the sixteenth to the nineteenth centuries. The book concludes by returning to the West African scene in the nineteenth century. No attempt is made to relate the exploits of European explorers, or to deal with the partition and colonization of Africa which followed, but a final chapter discusses the main influences upon African history as far as the present day.

It is expected that the teacher will have access to regional histories in the school library from which he can obtain more detailed knowledge for story-telling and explanation of the characters and events related only briefly here. Some questions suggested for the guidance of the teacher are included at the end.

A. J. W.

Contents

Acknowledgments

The author and publisher are grateful to the following for permission to reproduce the photographs on the pages indicated:

Aerofilms Ltd   65, 92, 105
Mike Andrews   96
Barnaby's Picture Library   91
Trustees of the British Museum   13 (right), 31, 46, 50 (both), 72 (bottom)
British Museum Natural History   36
Camera Press Ltd   19, 42, 48
J. Allan Cash   109
Crown Copyright   67
Mary Evans Picture Library   9, 28, 107 (both)
Mansell Collection   7, 26, 63, 72 (top), 74, 104, 112, 116, 120 (left), 123
Popperfoto Ltd   10, 12, 13 (left), 14, 15, 16, 17, 27, 44, 56, 58, 66, 71, 78, 90, 101, 103, 113, 114 (both), 117, 120 (right), 121, 126
Portuguese State Office   55
Radio Times Hulton Picture Library   11, 64, 122, 124, 129
Tanzanian Information Services   82, 87, 88

The illustration on page 51 is taken from the book of a Dutch geographer, Olphert Dapper (1668)

The extracts on pages 23, 70 and 133 are taken from *The African Past* by Basil Davidson. They are reproduced by permission of Longmans, Green and Co. Ltd

1 Islam in the north and west

In the last chapter of Book One we read how Arabs came to live on the east coast of Africa, and how this was partly due to the growth of the faith of Islam in Arab countries.

Islam had an even greater effect on North and West Africa. In this chapter we shall see how the new religion began, and some of the far-reaching developments that followed.

Islam

The Arabs in Arabia, until the sixth century, were divided into different tribes and worshipped many different gods. The most important god, however, respected by all, was believed to be a black meteorite stone that was kept in the temple at Mecca. Many people from all over Arabia used to come and kiss the stone, and the merchants of Mecca grew rich on their custom.

Mohammed, a Meccan camel-driver born in 570, made journeys as far as Palestine and met many people including Jews and Christians. He became convinced that there were not many

Early drawing of the Great Mosque at Mecca

gods, but only one God. When he began to preach in Mecca, however, the leaders of the city grew jealous and an attempt was made to take his life. Mohammed's escape, called the *Hijra*, from Mecca to Medina in 622 is taken as the starting point of the new religion.

This new faith, called *Islam*, which means 'submission' (to the will of God), condemned idolatry and taught all Moslems to treat one another as brothers, to be considerate to their families and to obey the rules of prayer. They must convert the world, by force if need be. Mohammed, indeed, declared a *jihad* or 'holy war'. The new faith began to spread like wildfire among the Arab tribes.

The first conquests of Islam

After Mohammed died in 632, his followers were inspired with his vision. The Arab tribes of the Yemen were united in an exultant resolve to spread the word of the Prophet through Arabia and beyond. To die in such a 'holy war' was to pass straight to Paradise. United under Mohammed's friend, Abu Bekr, who called himself the Khalif or 'Successor', the Arabs found that not even the hired armies of Byzantium could withstand the speed and ferocity of their northward advance.

Within four years of the Prophet's death, Syria was overrun. Soon Mesopotamia and Persia fell to Arab arms. Meanwhile a great Arab soldier, Amr-ibn-al-As, fell upon the rich fields of Egypt. By 642 the Arabs were rulers of the Lower Nile valley and Alexandria. A new phase in African history had begun.

Then the Arabs turned south, towards the Upper Nile. Here lived the Nubians, that fiercely independent people who had resisted the Romans, troubled the kingdom of Meroe, and fought with the armies of Aksum. These Nubians were the first people to check the all-conquering Arabs. They were skilful bowmen, and were as accustomed to desert fighting as the Arabs themselves. Moreover, following the example of the Aksumites two hundred years earlier, the Nubians had become Christians. They had been converted by missionaries from Egypt and Syria in about 550. Strengthened by a faith as inspiring as that of Islam itself, they resisted all Arab attempts at conquest.

In 652 the Arabs made a treaty with the Nubians. It was agreed that as long as Nubia continued to send gold and slaves down the Nile, as they had always done, the Arabs would leave their country alone. This treaty lasted for six hundred years.

The Sahara Desert

Al Mahgrib

Next the Arabs turned to the west, and soon conquered Libya as far as Cyrenaica.

Beyond Libya, they faced five hundred miles of waterless desert. This desert separated them from the fertile lowlands that stretch from Tunis to Morocco between the Atlas Mountains and the sea. This stretch of desert coast was to affect the whole future history of North and West Africa, because the Arabs in Egypt were never able properly to control the lands beyond it.

These lands, the fertile coastlands of the Atlas region, were called by the Arabs *Al Mahgrib*, which means 'The West'. Three centuries before, they had been rich provinces of the Roman Empire. Vandal raiders from Spain, as we have seen, had driven the Romans out and destroyed their cities. Now the country was inhabited by the original Berber population. They had mostly lost the Christianity of Roman times.

9

The Arabs now crossed the desert coast, and in 705, after thirty years of hard fighting, they were in control of Ifriq'iya (the old Roman province of 'Africa') and had founded a new capital at Tunis. They went on to occupy Numidia and Mauretania. Most of the Berbers were quickly converted to the new faith. In 711 an Arab army crossed the Straits of Gibraltar and invaded Spain.

Divisions in Islam

While these conquests were being made, a dispute about the leadership of Islam occurred.

The leader of Islam was known as the Khalif. The first Khalifs after the death of Mohammed were men, like Abu Bekr, who had known the Prophet. However, when the third Khalif, Othman, was assassinated in 655, the Arabs disagreed about who should be their next leader. Most of them decided

Mosque in Damascus, Syria

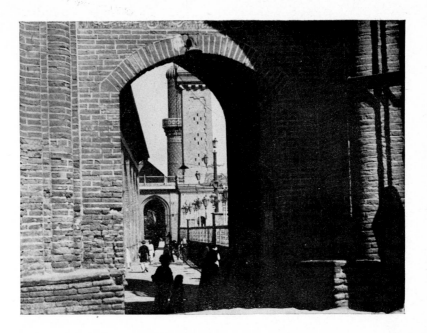

A gateway in Baghdad

to follow Mu'awiya, the governor of Damascus, who spoke Greek. Mu'awiya declared that his son would succeed him, thus founding a new dynasty which was called 'Umayyad'.

Many Moslems, however, did not like this new dynasty, and new groups were formed, some of whom, as we read in the last chapter, went to live in East Africa. This disagreement was important, because any Moslems who were faithful to Islam but also wanted to break free from the Arab Empire could say they belonged to a group which disagreed with the Umayyads.

Ninety years later, in 749, there was another quarrel among the Moslem leaders. The Umayyads were removed, and a new dynasty, called the Abbasids after their founder, Abdul Abbas, occupied the Khalifate.

The Abbasids made an important change. Until this time, the capital of the Arab Empire had been at Damascus in Syria, although Mecca in Arabia was always the religious centre of Islam. Now the Abbasids founded a new capital at Baghdad on the River Euphrates. Baghdad was a rich city, but it was much farther east. This helped the Moslems to make conquests in Afghanistan and northern India. However, it made it more difficult to hold together the vast Arab Empire in the west.

The isolation of the Mahgrib

In this way, the western part of North Africa, Al Mahgrib, became separated from the main Arab Empire for four reasons.

Firstly, five hundred miles of desert lay beyond Libya. Secondly, the Berber inhabitants were an independent-minded people who did not like to be ruled by Arabs. Thirdly, these inhabitants took advantage of the religious divisions of Islam to break away from the Khalifate. Fourthly, the new capital at Baghdad was too far away for effective control.

As a result, semi-independent Moslem states were formed in Ifriq'iya (Tunis), in Tahert in the central Mahgrib, in Morocco and in Spain. In this part of Africa the Berber people were all converted to Islam, and the Christianity that had existed there from Roman times was finally extinguished.

This was not so in Egypt. When the Arabs had conquered Egypt in 641, they had made an agreement with the Egyptian Christians that they could keep their own religion. This Egyptian or 'Coptic' church was to flourish in the centuries ahead, and even kept in touch with the Christians of the far-off highlands of Ethiopia, and of Nubia in the eastern Sudan.

Coptic Church near Tura, Egypt

Ethiopian Coptic cross

Ethiopian drawing of a saint: 17th century

Links with West Africa

Now you will remember that the Berber peoples of North Africa were linked with the Negro peoples of the Sudan by trade routes which crossed the Sahara. Arab religion and culture now spread along these routes. Arabs did not spread the faith of Islam by war alone. Once the Arab empires had been established, the work of converting was carried on by missionaries and traders.

Arabs from the east looked upon the Mahgrib, and even farther-off places like Spain in the north-west and the Sudan in the south-west, as colonies to be settled in. In the same way

13

Damascus: the burial ground where two of the wives of the Prophet and his daughter Fatima are interred

as they had colonized the east coast, Arabs came to settle in the west among the Spaniards, the Berbers and the Negroes. Arabic became the language of religion and of trade. Trade, just as much as conquest, brought the religion of Islam and the education of Arab civilization across the Sahara from the Mahgrib to the Sudan.

Before we come to events in the Sudan, however, we must follow their course in the Mahgrib a little further.

An empire in the Mahgrib

The Berbers in the Mahgrib had been converted to Islam, but neither they nor the Arab colonists liked to think that they were the subjects of the far-off Khalifate in Baghdad. They liked it less because that Khalifate was becoming more Persian and less Arab all the time.

About 900, therefore, a Berber tribe called Kutama started

a revolt. They did so in the name of a separate branch of Islam, which believed that the Abbasid Khalifs had no right to rule. Instead, the Berbers produced their own leader, who claimed to be the true descendant of Fatima, the wife of the Prophet.

Before long, these Fatimids were using the title of Khalif. They aimed to conquer the whole of Islam. Soon they were attacking Egypt, which fell in 969. Four years later a new capital on the Nile was built for the Fatimid Khalif Al Mu'izz. This capital was called Al Kahira, for which the modern name is Cairo.

The Fatimids were able to conquer Syria, but they went no farther than this. Before long, they were driven back by the Turks, who had arrived from the east and become Moslem. The Turks were powerful fighters, and in 1171 their great leader, Al Saladin, drove the Fatimids out of Egypt.

Meanwhile, the Berbers in the Mahgrib had already thrown off their allegiance to Cairo. The Fatimid Empire was at an end.

Damascus: the tomb of Saladin

The Almoravids

The great minaret of the Kulubiya Mosque at Marrakesh, built by the Almohads in the 12th century

Already, however, a new leader had appeared in the west. This happened among the Berber tribe of the Sahara region called Tuareg. The Tuareg were a fierce, hard-living people, whose menfolk wore the veiled head-dress which has made them famous.

In the eleventh century (about 1050), a Tuareg chief made the long pilgrimage to Mecca. Arrived there, he found that the true worship of Islam was a finer thing than the Berbers knew. Their own religious life had become slack. Determined to reform Islam in his country, he brought back with him an Arab teacher whose name was Ibn Yasin.

Ibn Yasin was not liked by the Tuareg. His rules for living were too strict. They burnt his dwelling and drove him away. However, Ibn Yasin was not daunted. With two companions, he went to a remote place and stayed in retreat for several months, preparing to lead a religious revival.

Such a place of retreat, or hermitage, is called in Arabic *ribat*, and Ibn Yasin's followers came to be called the Al Murabitin, or Almoravids. We do not know where the *ribat* was. Some say that it was an island in the Senegal River; others that

Islam in North Africa
1000–1100

it was an island in the sea, off the coast of Morocco.

His plans made, Ibn Yasin returned to the Mahgrib. Now his ideas spread like wildfire among the northern desert tribes. Men flocked to his banner. King Yahia of the Tuareg saw the opportunity to build an Almoravid empire. He decided to capture the whole Taodeni trail. In 1054 he took Audaghost at the southern end. Audaghost, in fact, was the northern outpost of Ghana. Two years later King Yahia marched north into Morocco. In 1057 he was killed in battle.

The next twenty years brought success to the Almoravids. They were now led by a great statesman, Abu Bekr. In the north, first Morocco and then Spain were conquered. In the south, Abu Bekr made an alliance with the Fulani, and conquered Ghana. Kumbi Saleh, their capital city, was captured in 1076. We shall hear more of this in the next chapter.

The end of the Berber Empires

The empire of the Almoravids did not last. When they became powerful over so large an area, their energy and the purity of their religion began to disappear. The Moroccan tribes of the Atlas Mountains did not like the Tuareg of the desert, and about 1125 they produced their own religious leader, Ibn Tumart. His followers, called Almohads—'people who say there is one God'—soon overran Morocco and Spain, and by 1159 they were rulers of the whole of the Mahgrib.

The Almohads were capable rulers, and made towns like Marrakesh and Fez into beautiful cities. But they were not able to impose unity on the Berber tribes for long. After a hundred years (by 1250), the Mahgrib had broken up again into its tribal parts. Finally there were the three countries that we know today as Tunisia, Algeria and Morocco.

The Negro peoples of the Sudan formed no part of these Berber states. Once more the connecting link was reduced to the age-old trans-Saharan trade routes.

However, for a short time in the eleventh century, the Almoravid 'explosion' had brought the Negroes into touch with Berber government and, what is more important, the religion of Islam. In the twenty years from 1070 to 1090, Islam came to the Negro states of Ghana on the Upper Niger, of Songhai at Gao, and of Kanem north of Lake Chad. The Hausa alone resisted the new faith for a time. In the next chapters we follow the stories of these Negro states.

A Tuareg tribesman

2 Old Ghana

The old kingdom of Ghana was quite different from the Ghana of today. It was in a different place, north of the Niger, and inhabited by different people. There are links between the two, as we shall see, which is why the present state of Ghana was given its name; but these links are frail.

The kingdom of Old Ghana

How Ghana began

One of the oldest trans-Saharan trails crossed the desert from Morocco to the Middle and Upper Niger. This was the Taodeni trail. It had three advantages. It was shorter than the others because the Niger, flowing north into the desert, meets its southern end. The Sahara could be crossed in six weeks by the Taodeni. Secondly, it avoided the harsh terrain and brigand-infested ravines of the Hoggar Mountains. Finally, it linked the rich, salt-bearing ground south of the Moroccan Atlas with the gold of the Upper Niger region.

Salt and gold, in this part of Africa, were the great objects of trade from ancient times. Compared with them slaves and,

Berber riding camel

later, cloth were less important. Gold had been eagerly sought in Europe since Roman times. Europe had little gold, and the treasures of Egypt were used up. Some gold was found in the east, most of it coming from the Sudan. From the early Middle Ages, West African gold gleamed on the crowns and in the coffers of the popes and kings of Christendom.

Out of this trade were born the Negro states of the Sudan. The Mandingo in particular lived across the trade route between the salt supplies of the desert and the gold resources of the Senegal-Niger watershed.

During the first few centuries A.D., in the time of the Roman Empire, the Mandingo were simple farmers and herdsmen. They lived in small villages of simple huts and most of their tools were of stone. They allowed Berber traders to pass through their country in peace. They watched them and learned from them, so that in time they began to take part in the trade themselves. The Mandingo bought gold from the forest tribes to the south, and traded it with travellers from the north. From these Berber travellers they bought salt and other goods.

Now some of the Mandingo communities began to grow richer. One of them, in late Roman times, became the kingdom of Ghana. Though a small chiefdom at first, its ruler could afford to pay and equip soldiers, and so have order in the kingdom and power over neighbours. Traders could be compelled to pay taxes. In such a way, all the nations of the world have built up their power.

About the end of the Roman period, perhaps in the fifth century, the camel was introduced into North Africa from Arabia. This made a great difference. The desert was drying up and horses could no longer survive the hot, thirsty journey. Now, with the camel, trade increased again. More Berber traders came, their camel caravans laden with goods. When the Romans were driven from North Africa, the Berbers were free to develop the trade themselves.

Berber kings in Ghana

Because of their wealth and their camel transport, some Berber traders were able to become powerful in Mandingo country, just as, in recent times, Arab traders were able to make themselves chiefs in East Africa. In this way, they could organize the trade more to their own profit. Instead of paying taxes, they received taxes themselves.

In this way, the Mandingo state of Ghana was ruled by Berber trader chiefs for over four hundred years. Mandingo traditions say that they had 'white' or Berber rulers from about 400 to about 630. Then came a change of dynasty, and a new line of Berber kings ruled until about 850.

Of the history of Ghana during this time we know little. Probably the most important development was the increasing use of iron for all kinds of implements and weapons. The gold trade also continued to grow. Towards the end of the Berber period, in 730, an Arab astronomer and geographer, Al Fazari, put the kingdom of Ghana on a map, and wrote of it simply as 'the land of gold'.

In civilization, however, Ghana was still backward. The chief's capital town was still built of mud houses. The art of writing was not known among the people, and there were no schools. Travellers brought news of the great Prophet and his teaching, but few were converted and the old pagan beliefs were still supreme.

The Soninke kings

About 850, a revolution took place in Ghana. The people of the country rose up against their rulers and put a Negro dynasty, of the Soninke clan, upon the throne. The Berber king was killed, but there is no story to say why. Probably the Moslem conquest of the Mahgrib had upset the Berber states north of the Sahara. This might have reduced trade across the desert for a time, and weakened Berber control of the Sudan.

Many Berbers from Ghana fled west to Tekrur. We believe that there, by mixing with the Negro Tucolor and Wolof tribes, they formed the Fulani people.

The Soninke kings ruled Ghana for two hundred years. It was a time of growing prosperity. Trade revived, and then the Negro people themselves reaped all the benefit. Towns grew larger, and the ruler now lived in a fixed capital called Al Ghaba. Though the Soninke were still pagans, so many Moslems now traded in the country that the separate town of Kumbi Saleh was built for them a few miles from Al Ghaba itself. The Ghana Empire was extended to the Senegal River in the west and to the great bend of the Niger in the east. Its southern boundary was in the hills of the watershed, while to the north the frontier town of Audaghost looked out across scrub country of the desert fringe.

The fame of Ghana spread to far away Arabia. Arab travellers made the long journey to see the country. About 970 one of them, Ibn Hawqal, reported that the Emperor of Ghana was 'the richest in the world because of his gold'. At the end of the Soninke period a great geographer, Al Bekri, described the gold ornaments on the uniforms and weapons of servants and guards at the royal court at Al Ghaba. The Emperor's horse was tethered to a gold nugget weighing thirty pounds. His robes were of oriental silk. Great honour was done him at his court. In his army of 200,000 men, 40,000 were bowmen. The palace was built of stone, and twelve stone mosques stood in the neighbouring Moslem town of Kumbi Saleh.

Most of the people were still pagan, but Moslems, because they could read and write, held important posts in the government. These Moslems were Negroes. Berber traders came and went, but they had no power.

However, this was suddenly to change. Out of the north came the whirlwind of a new Berber conquest.

The Almoravids

In the last chapter we read how the Almoravid religious revival sprang up in the Mahgrib. In 1065 Ibn Yasin himself led an army to the frontier town of Audaghost and, wrote El Bekri, 'took it by storm, carrying off all they found there'. Fifteen years later, in 1069, Abu Bekr declared a *jihad* or 'holy war' against Ghana, and a Berber army swept across the desert. In 1076 Kumbi was taken and sacked, and the Soninke Empire was no more.

This time, Berber rule in Ghana did not last for long. The Almoravids, as we shall see, were to be driven out by a new Negro uprising after only seventy years. But these seventy years were to have deep and lasting effects on the history of West Africa.

First of these effects was the spread of Islam. The Soninke kings had been pagan. The new rulers were Moslems, and many of the people were persuaded to follow the Prophet. The new faith spread, not only in Ghana, but down the Niger for a thousand miles. We must not suppose that all the people became converted in a short time, but by 1100 Islam was the strongest religion throughout the Negro peoples of the western Sudan. With it came the birth of education and learning.

The second effect of the Almoravid conquest was the movement of peoples. Some tribes, rather than accept the new faith, and fearing the onslaught of the Almoravid armies, fled southeast from Ghana across the Niger. It is possible that the ancestors of the Akan people of modern Ghana were among these groups who moved south from old Ghana to escape the *jihad*. Others, however, say that the Akan came from the north.

Lastly, the Empire of Ghana never recovered from the conquest.

The decline of Ghana

The fact is that the peoples of Ghana had never been strongly united. Even under the Soninke kings there had been quarrels. The Mandingo were divided between the Soninke clan in the north and the Walinke in the south. Both had disputes with subject Berber tribes such as the Lemta of Audaghost. Soon after the conquest, these quarrels broke out again.

Two rival groups opposed each other in Central Ghana. West of Kumbi were the Sosso, whose king Sumanguru plundered Kumbi itself in 1203. But the Sosso feared the kingdom of Kangaba in the south. When the chief of Kangaba died, Sumanguru tried to kill all the chief's twelve sons so that none should succeed him. Eleven of them were indeed put to death, but the twelfth was a sickly child, and the soldiers spared his life. His name was Sundiata.

For twenty-five years till his death in 1235, Sumanguru was the strongest chief in Ghana, but his rule was not complete and the empire continued to crumble. Indeed, Ghana was no longer an empire at all by 1240, when Sundiata, who had been living in exile farther down the Niger, arrived at the head of an army and defeated the Sosso on the decisive field of Krina.

There is much to be told of Sundiata, but it belongs to the story of Mali, of whose empire he was the founder king.

The King of Ghana can put two hundred thousand warriors in the field, more than forty thousand being armed with bow and arrow.

When he gives audience to his people, to listen to their complaints and set them to rights, he sits in a pavilion around which stand ten pages holding shields and gold-mounted swords; and on his right hand are the sons of the princes of the empire, splendidly clad and with gold plaited into their hair. The governor of the city is seated on the ground in front of the king, and all around him are his viziers in the same position. The gate of the chamber is guarded by dogs of an excellent breed, who wear collars of gold and silver. The beginning of a royal audience is announced by the beating of a kind of drum which they call *deba*, made of a long piece of hollowed wood. The people gather when they hear this sound.

The King of Ghana exacts the right of one *dinar* of gold on each donkey-load of salt that enters his country. The best gold in the country comes from Ghiaru, a town situated in a country that is densely populated by Negroes and covered with villages. All pieces of gold found in the mines of the empire belong to the sovereign, although he lets the public have the gold dust that everybody knows about; without this precaution, gold would become so abundant as practically to lose its value.

Al Bekri

3 The Empire of Mali

The empire which Sundiata founded on his thirteenth-century conquests was to be much greater in extent than Ghana had been, and much wealthier. And while Ghana, in spite of the Almoravid conquest, was still mostly a heathen country, Mali was ruled by Moslems from the beginning. Many of its people became devout followers of the faith.

The Empire of Mali

Origins

Little is known of Mali in the time before Sundiata. It began as a small Negro chiefdom on the Upper Niger to the south-west of Ghana. The chief's village was at Niani on the Sankara, a small tributary river. There was gold in the country. The long-established presence of Berber trading settlements perhaps explains why the people of Mali held to Islam after the Almoravid government was overthrown. It may also explain why the Sosso were jealous and afraid of the Mali kingdom of Kangaba.

We have seen in the last chapter how Sundiata became the leader of this kingdom.

Sundiata is one of the great figures of history. Lame and sickly as a child, he had overcome his difficulties and had grown to manhood as a great warrior and hunter. So popular was he among the people, who knew that he was of royal descent, that he aroused the jealousy of the king. Fearing for his life, he went into exile, far away towards Timbuktu.

In 1240, however, oppressed by new threats from the Sosso, the king fled from Niani. Now the people called on Sundiata to come back and lead them.

As soon as he was back in Niani, Sundiata raised an army. Undeterred by grief at his mother's death on the eve of his departure, he marched north into the heart of Mandingo country. He was welcomed by the people as a liberator. Meeting Sumanguru and the Sosso on the decisive field of Krina, he won a complete victory. Sumanguru was taken captive, and died soon afterwards.

Before long, Kumbi was also taken, and Sundiata was proclaimed Emperor—no longer of Ghana, but of Mali. A new capital was made at Bamako, some way down the Niger from Niani, and Kumbi, already shattered by two conquests in ten years, fell into decay.

During the remaining fifteen years of his life, Sundiata's armies advanced the frontiers of his empire in every direction, especially down the Niger to the east, and down the Senegal to the west.

Sundiata died in 1255. He may have been shot by an arrow from an angry crowd, but others say he was accidentally drowned in the Sankara River.

Though some of the people of Ghana had taken to Islam in Almoravid times, it was only now, under Sundiata and the other Moslem rulers who followed him, that the conversion became widespread.

The Mandingo and other Negro peoples of the Niger took to Islam with a fervour that amazed visitors from far afield. They were linked more and more closely with the rest of the Moslem world. There was the trade with the Berber states north of the desert. More directly, trade routes went to the eastern Sudan beyond the Shari. A few Moslems from Mali even used to make the pilgrimage to faraway Mecca. Indeed, Mali was no isolated state. One of the great empires of the whole world in its day, its people had a great sense of brotherhood with the rest of the Islamic world.

The most famous pilgrim from Mali to Mecca was the greatest of its rulers after Sundiata. This was Mansa Kankan Musa.

Kankan Musa

The ninth ruler of Mali after Sundiata, Musa was the great-grandson of the founder's sister. He ruled from 1307 to 1332. During his reign the frontiers of Mali were once again advanced, until the emperor's word was law as far as Cape Verde on the Atlantic coast. To the east, though resisted by the Mossi tribes of the Black Volta, Mali extended its power over the whole Niger bend, and even down the river beyond Gao.

When Kankan Musa made his pilgrimage to Mecca in 1324, he passed through Cairo. By this time, Cairo had grown to be more important than Baghdad, and was one of the great

Artist's impression of a caravan on its way to Mecca: 18th century

View of Cairo, showing the Citadel Mosque

cities of the world. Even here, however, the size and the rich
finery of Musa's caravan made a powerful impression. The
people and rulers of Cairo marvelled at his retinue of sixty
thousand men, his eighty camels, each loaded with gold, and
the staves covered with beaten gold with which his five hundred
personal servants were equipped.

Musa's visit was talked about for years afterwards. It was the
first time that most people in Egypt realized that, beyond the
sunbaked and dusty plains of the central Sudan, there flowed
another great river, as great as the Nile; and that on its banks

there throve another kingdom rich in gold. What was more, marvel of marvels, its people were followers of the Prophet.

Because Cairo was a centre of Mediterranean trade, rumours of Mali reached Europe before long. The Empire of Mali is written on one of the earliest maps of Africa since Ptolemy, which was drawn by an Italian in 1375.

The pilgrimage to Mecca took three years. It is plain how well-governed Mali was, that its ruler could be away for so long. Meanwhile the armies of Mali continued their conquests. Musa returned to find that his general Sagama-Dir had captured Gao, the capital of the Songhai people, in 1325. Musa passed through Gao in triumph on his way home.

A traveller's sketch of Timbuktu

Timbuktu	Impressed by what he had seen in Cairo and Mecca, Musa devoted the last years of his life to improving the cities of his country. The earliest flat-roofed brick-built houses were probably built in Timbuktu and Gao at this time, and new mosques were raised up. One, the Sankuru mosque at Timbuktu, was designed by Ishaq-es-Saheli, a Berber from southern Spain.

Originally a Tuareg settlement, Timbuktu had begun as a trading town. Situated at the northernmost point of the Niger bend, it has been called 'the port of the Sudan in the Sahara', where river canoe and desert camel meet. As formerly at Kumbi, gold from the south and salt from the north were exchanged in its markets. During the next century Timbuktu and another city called Djenne, farther up the Niger, became important centres of learning. We shall read of this in the next chapter, but their rise to greatness belongs to the days of the Empire of Mali.

The wealth of Mali	Mansa Kankan Musa died in 1352. At the time of his death, Mali was at the height of its wealth and power. These rested on three things.

First of all, Mali controlled the richest gold deposits in West Africa. Now that the mines of Nubia, exploited for centuries by the Egyptians, were used up, the resources of the Niger-Senegal watershed were the richest of the known world. Gold from Mali found its way all over the Middle East and Europe. There the wars of the Cross had stimulated trade. The growth of towns in Europe during the Middle Ages was increasing the demand for gold.

Secondly, Mali now controlled the southern end of two of the great trans-Saharan camel trails, whereas Ghana had only controlled one. The first of these was the Taodeni trail, which went north through the western desert to Sijilmasa. On this route lay the rich salt mines of Taghaza oasis. There, salt was cut from the ground in blocks. It was even used to build houses. More or less independent, Taghaza was often in dispute between the Negro empires in the south and Morocco in the north. The real northern outpost of Mali was Walata. Here travellers coming south from Taghaza had to be met by guides before they were allowed to enter the town.

The other trail controlled by Mali at the southern end was the Ghadames trail from Tunis, through the Hoggar to Gao.

*Trade routes
across the Sahara*

Lastly, the government of Mali was efficient and well-organized. Order and peace are essential if trade is to flourish. It is plain from Arab accounts that order and peace reigned in the Empire of Mali under Mansa Musa. The most important of these accounts was written by the great Arab geographer, Ibn Batuta.

Ibn Batuta's account

Ibn Batuta was a Moroccan Arab who travelled in many Moslem countries, writing about what he saw. He went to India and China as well as to Africa.

In 1352 he made a journey from Morocco to Mali, crossing the western Sahara from Sijilmasa to Walata. He spent three years in Mali, most of it in the capital, but he also visited Timbuktu and Gao.

Three things impressed Ibn Batuta. The first was the respect for law and order. The country was organized in provinces, each controlled by a governor or *Ferba*. Below him were *Mocrifs* who controlled towns and villages. Law was strictly enforced. 'The Negroes are of all peoples those who most abhor injustice,' wrote Ibn Batuta. Travellers could move about in safety. If one

A page of the Koran: Egyptian, 14th century

should die, his goods were taken care of until someone came to claim them.

The second was the devoutness of the people, especially the wealthy and educated, in worshipping according to the faith of Islam. The mosques were full, and a worshipper who arrived late might not find a place. Clean white clothes were worn on Fridays, even by the poor. Children were made to learn the Koran by heart. There were, of course, many pagans in Mali, the Moslems being mostly in the big towns.

Lastly, Ibn Batuta noted the respect shown to the king or

Mansa, who was surrounded with great pomp. Audiences were held on a raised platform under a tree in the palace forecourt. The platform was carpeted with silk and covered with cushions. The king appeared, walking slowly, wearing a gold skull-cap and a red velvet tunic of cloth from Europe. In front came musicians with two-stringed guitars, and in the rear followed three hundred armed slaves. Drums, trumpets and bugles were sounded.

A subject who wished to see the king had to wear old clothes drawn up to the knees. He would approach, bowing low, and would knock the ground with his elbows. When spoken to by the king, he would throw dust over his back as a sign of submission.

Ibn Batuta saw how the Niger flowed eastwards, and wondered whether it later joined the Nile. When he returned home he drew a map showing the Empire of Mali; and after this, Mali appeared on European maps of the world until the sixteenth century.

The decline of Mali

Although Ibn Batuta did not know it, Mali slowly began to decline in the years after his visit. No ruler as great as Musa succeeded to the throne. Soon there was a dispute between rival claimants, which led to civil war. A series of weak rulers followed. Gao claimed its independence. After 1400, Mali suffered increasingly from attacks by the Tuareg in the north, the Wolof in the west, and the Mossi in the south.

Finally the country was overthrown by the armies of Songhai in 1513. In the next chapter we shall read about the growth of this new and even greater empire.

4 Songhai

While first Ghana, and then Mali had been growing into strong states centred on the Upper Niger, another people had been building a new state along the Middle Niger.

These were the Negro people called the Songhai.

The Empire of Songhai

How the Songhai kingdom began

About the seventh century when, far up the Niger to the west, the kingdom of Ghana was growing strong under its first Berber kings, a Negro tribe called the Songhai moved from their homeland around the Bussa rapids, up to the Middle Niger.

From the rapids at Bussa in the east to Bamako in the west, the Niger flows through a thousand miles of dry, healthy country, without a single waterfall or rapid to break its even flow. It was to be the destiny of the Songhai to make this thousand miles their own.

The Songhai reached Gao about 650. There they found themselves at the southern end of the ancient cart trail through the Hoggar grasslands to Ghadames.

The Berbers of the Lemta tribe, who used this trail, fought the Songhai newcomers, and conquered them about 700. The Berber chief was called Za Aliamen. His descendants, called the Za kings, ruled the Songhai for over six hundred years. During this time, through intermarriage, they became partly Negro, and formed the Songhai into a strong nation.

In 1009, Za Kosoi became a Moslem, taught by Berber traders from the north. All the kings after him were Moslem, and the new religion slowly began to spread among the people.

Mali conquers Songhai

By this time Gao had become a large town, and its trade began to rival that of Timbuktu. At last, as we have seen, it was captured by Musa's army in 1325. The Za king was killed, and his two small sons were taken away as hostages.

For about fifty years, Gao and half the Songhai kingdom were ruled by the emperor of Mali. A palace and a fine new mosque were built in the town. But after Musa's death, the Songhai slowly stopped paying tribute to Mali. The two princes escaped from Timbuktu, and went back. The eldest started a new line of kings, giving up the old title of 'Za', and calling himself 'Sonni' instead.

Mali finally gave up Gao in 1435 because of Berber attacks. The Songhai managed to fight off the invaders, but the Berbers captured Timbuktu, and from this time Mali began to decline.

Sonni Ali

Mali's decline was Songhai's opportunity. The Negro peoples of the Niger did not like Berber rule. The rulers of Mali had not been able to keep the Berbers back, and now it was the turn of the Songhai.

In 1464 the governor of Timbuktu appealed to Gao for help in throwing off Berber rule. The king of Songhai at that time was Sonni Ali. When he reached Timbuktu he found that the Berbers had fled. The learned men of the schools and the university, however, made it clear that they feared the Songhai just as much, and did not want them in the city. This made Sonni Ali so angry that he destroyed many buildings, and hunted to death many of the citizens.

In fact Sonni Ali, though a great leader and fighter, was a hot-tempered and cruel man. Fortunately he had a wise general called Mohammed Ali Bekr, who knew how to wait until his master's temper had cooled before asking him a question.

Sonni Ali ruled from 1464 to 1492. After a siege of seven years, he also captured the other of Mali's university towns, Djenne. This time he treated the schoolmen more kindly. For a time, also, he held Walata in the desert. He even tried to build a canal from Lake Faquibine to Walata, but it was never finished. He fought long wars against the Mossi in the south and the Fulani in the north-east. When he died, the Songhai Empire was already stronger than Mali.

Askia the Great

Now Sonni Ali's great minister, Mohammed Ali Bekr, decided to make himself king. He fought and defeated Sonni Ali's sons, and rode back to Gao victorious. When told that Mohammed was now king, Sonni Ali's daughters in the palace cried out 'A si kyi a!'—'He isn't!' Mohammed heard of this and, laughing, declared that 'Askia' should be his title. So it was, and of the kings who followed him as well.

This man, even more than Mansa Musa of Mali, deserves the title of 'great'. Above all he was a great soldier. Attacking Mali in 1501, his armies conquered it after a long war, and extended the power of Songhai as far as the Atlantic coast where the Senegal and Gambia Rivers meet the sea. To the north he controlled for a time the salt mines of Taghaza, regarded for centuries by the Berbers as their own. To the east, he subdued the Hausa states around Katsina, and captured Kano (1513). He fought and conquered the Fulani and Tuareg of Aïr. A Negro colony at the Berber town of Agades survives to this day.

Besides this, however, Askia was a great administrator. He brought peace and good government to the whole of the western Sudan. The people of his cities had no fear of thieves; children could safely be sent to buy in the market; and travellers were safe on the road. Judges were honest and respected. Education was encouraged, and many books were bought and sold.

Lastly Askia, unlike Sonni Ali, was a strict Moslem. Wishing, perhaps, to do better than Musa a hundred and fifty years before, he made in 1495 a *hadj* or pilgrimage to Mecca. In his huge caravan were five hundred horsemen and a thousand foot soldiers, and his baggage train included three hundred thousand pieces of gold for expenses and gifts on the journey.

Askia Mohammed lived to be ninety-seven years old. He reigned for so long that his sons grew tired of waiting for their turn to rule. They rebelled against him in 1528, and Askia was exiled for three years. But the rebel princes could not govern well. Askia came back to Gao, and ruled until his death in 1538.

The Moroccan wars

The kings after Askia Mohammed used the same title, but none was as capable. His sons quarrelled, until Askia Ishak I (1539–1549) restored order. With the death of Askia Daud in 1582, trouble broke out again.

Worst of all, war now began with Morocco across the desert. The Moroccans had long been waiting to seize the gold trade, and the quarrels in Songhai, together with a victory over their other enemies, the Portuguese, gave them their chance. In 1585 the great Shereef of Morocco, Muley Muhammed El Mansur, captured the salt mines of Taghaza. He then sent an army across the desert to attack Gao itself.

After the terrible desert journey of five months, only two thousand of the Moroccan army survived. None the less, in 1591 they defeated the Askia's army of twenty-eight thousand in the historic battle of Tondibi. Their victory was due to the use of firearms. It was the first time that gunpowder had been used in the Sudan. The fire-locks and muzzle-loading cannon, brought from Spain, were too much for the bows and arrows and spears of the Songhai.

For twenty years the Shereef's army terrorized central Songhai. Gao was occupied, and Timbuktu was sacked, many of its books were destroyed and its educated men taken away to Marrakesh as slaves.

Tsetse-fly

However, the war brought little profit to Morocco. The Moroccan army failed to reach the gold mines of Wangara and Asante. These lay in the forest belt, and in trying to find them, many soldiers died of malaria and dysentery, while their horses were killed by the tsetse-fly. It was difficult to send more soldiers across the desert.

In 1618 the Shereef of Morocco abandoned the Sudan.

The end of the empires in the Sudan

The damage had been done; civilized government in Songhai had been destroyed. The Askias withdrew, with many of their own people of pure Songhai tribe, down the Niger to their own homeland in the Dendi region. The cities of Gao, Timbuktu and Djenne declined in importance.

The Moroccan soldiers stayed on the Niger and made

West Africa in the 17th century after the Moroccan wars

governments of their own, which lasted for one hundred and fifty years. But it was bad government: disorder and unhappiness returned to the country.

The battle of Tondibi therefore marked a turning point in the history of the Niger. The growth of civilization in the western Sudan was halted. Little progress was made in the next three hundred years. When the Scottish explorer Mungo Park journeyed down the Niger as far as Bussa in 1805, he found the country divided up into small states, often quarrelling with each other. The age of the great empires was over.

In the next two chapters we shall read of what had been happening in other parts of West Africa.

West African Time Chart to 1600

Date	Ghana	Mali	Songhai
A.D.			
100	Small Mandingo chiefdoms on Upper Niger and Senegal.		
200			
300			
400	First Berber conquest.	Independent Mande tribes.	
500			
600	Second Berber conquest.		Songhai Negroes move up Niger to Gao.
700			Berber conquest. Za kings begin.
800	Al Fazari calls Ghana 'land of gold' Revolution. Soninke kings begin.	Mali a small part of the Ghana kingdom.	
900			
1000	*Ghana kingdom at greatest extent.* Almoravid invasion. Ghana conquered 1069.		Za kings converted to Islam.
1100	Islam in Ghana. Collapse of Almoravid rule.		
1200	Sosso dominance under Sumanguru. End of Ghana.	Battle of Krina. Sundiata establishes Empire of Mali.	
1300		Islam spreads along the Niger.	Gao conquered by Mali in 1325.
1400		Musa's *hadj* to Mecca. Visit of Ibn Batuta (1352). *Greatest time of Mali's power and wealth.*	Songhai regains independence.
1500		Songhai conquest. Collapse of Mali.	Sonni Ali creates Empire of Songhai. Askia conquers Mali.
1600			*Greatest extent of Songhai.* Moroccan wars. Collapse of Songhai.

5 Kanem, Bornu and the Hausa states

In the last three chapters we have followed the rise and fall of three West African empires—Ghana, Mali and Songhai. These empires were centred on the Niger. Farther east meanwhile had grown the great kingdom of Bornu, which had grown out of the earlier state of Kanem. Bornu and Kanem were centred on Lake Chad.

Between Bornu and the Niger empires lay the Hausa states, which traded with these countries and also with North Africa, using the Ghadames trail.

We shall now see how Bornu and the Hausa states, which cover what is today Northern Nigeria, came into being.

Kanem—an early kingdom of the Sudan

From Chapter 8 in Book One you will remember how, during the last centuries B.C., Berber peoples from the north-east were moving west across the Tibesti Plateau towards Lake Chad. As the Sahara became dry, these Berbers sought for better grazing and water. They were pleased to find Lake Chad and the rivers flowing into it.

By A.D. 700 the Berbers, notably the Zaghawa, one of the strongest tribes, controlled the Sudan from Nubia in the east to Chad in the west. Around Lake Chad lived agricultural Negro people. The Berbers conquered them because, being nomads, they were better at fighting than the peaceful farmers.

Soon this huge, loose empire split up. About 800 one section, the Beni Sef, led by a chief called Dougou, founded the state of Kanem east of Lake Chad. Dougou's 'Sefawa' dynasty was to last a thousand years, so becoming one of the longest dynasties in the history of the world. The Beni Sef slowly intermarried with the Negro inhabitants, and Kanem became a Negro state. The title of the Kanem 'Sefawa' kings was *Mai*. Mai Selma (1193–1210) was the first Negro ruler of Kanem. He governed with a council of twelve, who were mostly members of the royal family.

Meanwhile, Islam was spreading through Egypt and North Africa. News of the new religion reached westward across the Sudan. In 1097 Mai Umme Jilmi became the first Moslem ruler of Kanem.

This was thirty years after the Almoravid conquest of

Ghana, far away to the west. The Niger states were converted to Islam from the north; the Chad states received it from the east.

The growth of Bornu

Kanem was a large, unwieldy state. After 1200, when it reached its greatest extent under Mai Dunama Dibbalemi, there were quarrels and civil war. The people found it difficult to resist attacks by the Bulala, a Berber tribe of the central Sudan.

West of Lake Chad, however, was the country of Bornu. Bornu was friendly with the Hausa states; some historians even regard it as having been one of the Hausa states, about which we shall read below. To this country the Kanuri (people of Kanem) came in search of new lands. Already by 1200 the Mai sometimes used the title of 'King of Kanem and Master of Bornu'.

It took over a hundred years for the Sefawa kings to build their new state and establish peaceful government, but by the time of Mai Ali Gazi (1473–1501) it was done. Ali Gazi built a new capital at Ngazargamu, which you can see on the map.

Kanem, Bornu and the Hausa Bokwoi about 1550

40

Thus by 1500 old Kanem east of Lake Chad no longer existed, and the strongest state in the Chad area was the Moslem kingdom of Bornu. Apart from Songhai, the last of the Niger empires, Bornu was the strongest kingdom in the whole of the western Sudan.

It was troubled, however, by the growing power of the Hausa states. We must now go back and see how these states had come into being.

The Hausa states

Some time around A.D. 800, which was the time when Ghana was beginning on the Upper Niger, and when Kanem was being formed under the Sefawa kings east of Chad, a group of towns grew up south of the desert between Lake Chad and the Niger bend.

This country was at the southern end of the Ghadames trail from Tunis. It was almost certainly for reasons of trade that these towns began. By 1200 there were seven of them, known as the Hausa Bokwoi. *Hausa* was the name of the language spoken by the people of these towns.

A legend says that Abuyazidu, a prince of Baghdad in far-off Persia (more probably he was the son of a Berber chieftain in eastern Bornu), quarrelled with his father and journeyed to western Bornu. At Daura he found that the people could not draw water because of a snake that lived in the well. Abuyazidu killed the snake. After that he married the Queen of Daura, and his six sons became the rulers of the other six Hausa towns. These were Kano and Katsina, trading communities; Zaria, a slave market; Rano, a craft centre; Gobir, a northern garrison against desert tribes; and Biram, between Kano and Lake Chad.

Although the story of the snake is a legend, these are the names of the original Hausa states. Probably the story represents an invasion of the Hausa country, led by a warrior called Abuyazidu, from ancient Bornu. Later new Hausa towns sprang up as trade increased. These were known as the Hausa Banza, and included Nupe, Yaura and even Ilorin, a Yoruba town south of the Niger.

Kano

The Hausa Bokwoi did not govern the people of the surrounding country. Each town had strong, high walls and mainly looked after its own defences and trade. Each was independent of the others, and there were sometimes wars between them.

41

Scene at a gateway of the walled city of Kano, Nigeria

The most important were Kano and Katsina, and by 1300 Kano was the strongest of all. Its king had a fine army, with mighty troops of horsemen.

This was the time when Mali was powerful on the Upper Niger. It was probably through the influence of Mali that some of the Hausa people were converted to Islam. We have read of Mansa Musa's pilgrimage to Mecca in 1325. He returned along the Ghadames trail. The Hausa were used to pilgrims. In fact Yaji, king of Kano in 1350, was a Moslem, although his successor was once more a pagan.

By 1400 Kano was a great city. Learned men from Mali went to stay there, and education spread among the wealthier people. Mosques were built. The law of the Koran was established, and the city was well governed.

Nevertheless, Islam was not so strongly established in the Hausa towns as it was in Mali and Songhai, or even in Bornu. From time to time the rulers were pagan, and many of the people were never Moslem. Pagan rites accompanied the enthronement of the Hausa kings. Indeed the Hausa, who occupy the north-west of modern Nigeria, were not properly converted to Islam until the Fulani *jihad* of the nineteenth century (see Chaper 15).

Bornu and Songhai dominate Hausaland

By 1500, Songhai was a powerful empire on the Upper Niger. Bornu, as we have seen, was a great kingdom south-west of Lake Chad. Between them lay the rich Hausa towns. Clearly, both Bornu and Songhai would want to control the Hausa.

The Bornu attempt came first. Under Mai Idris (1507–29), Bornu conquered eastern Hausaland, and became its overlord. Each town had to pay taxes to the Mai every year.

Meanwhile Askia Mohammed of Songhai was advancing eastward from Gao. We have seen how in 1513 he subdued the western Hausa, and captured Katsina and Kano. The Hausa towns were left desolate by the invasion.

The Hausa regain independence

Soon, however, the Hausa towns were able to throw off foreign domination. They succeeded for three reasons.

In the first place Askia the Great, blind at the end of his long reign, quarrelled with his sons. The governor of the Hausa town of Kebbi, who was called Kanta, took the opportunity to lead a Hausa revolt. Both the Songhai administrators and the Bornu tax-gatherers were driven out of Hausaland. Kanta, however, was killed fighting, and was unable to enjoy his triumph.

The second reason was the defeat of Songhai by the army of Morocco in 1591. We have read about the battle of Tondibi in the previous chapter. Songhai never recovered from this conquest, and the Hausa were thenceforth safe from attack in the west.

Thirdly, there took place the decline of Bornu. This did not happen at once. For a time Bornu recovered its power under Mai Idris Alooma. Greatest of the kings of Bornu, Idris Alooma had a fine army of noble cavalry. Both horses and men wore chain armour and brightly-coloured cloaks, and carried decorated shields and lances. Slaves and peasants, armed with spears and bows and arrows, came behind. With this well-trained force, Idris Alooma recovered power and reconquered Kano.

Forty years later, however, the kingdom of Bornu began to weaken under attacks of the Tuareg in the north and the Jukun in the south. The Jukun were a nomadic tribe who lived along the Upper Benue. Their raids troubled Bornu and Kanem until after 1700.

However, by the time that the rule of Bornu was thrown off by the Hausa, Kano was in decay after so many wars, and Katsina, now the strongest of the Hausa towns, controlled the Sahara trade.

Thus we see that the Hausa kept their independence in the end not so much through their own strength as because of the troubles and divisions of their enemies. They were good fighters, but they were never united enough to be a strong military power. They were still quarrelling among themselves when the force of the Fulani *jihad* (Chapter 15) broke upon them in 1804, and they were completely overrun.

Hausa horsemen

6 The forest kingdoms

South and west of the Lower Niger lies the country of the rain forest. This country was not reached by the power of Bornu to the north-east, or by that of the Hausa states to the north, or by that of Songhai to the north-west.

Thus the people who lived here were less influenced by Berber stock, and not at all by the Islamic religion. The kingdoms which developed around Ife, Oyo and Benin were Negro kingdoms. Even here, however, there were some contacts with foreign blood and culture.

The forest kingdoms
1600–1800

Northern limit of rain forest

0   150   300
Miles

The Yoruba

Among the most numerous and important of the peoples living in the forest country by A.D. 1000 were the Yoruba.

We are not sure where the Yoruba came from. Like other peoples of the region, they have a tradition that they came from the east. They have some Hamitic blood, and it is likely that some of their ancestors were Berbers or Hamites from the Nile and perhaps, long before that, from Ethiopia and Arabia. These ancestors were, we believe, among those tribes which migrated west and south as the Sahara slowly dried up until, crossing the Shari River, they mixed with the Negro peoples of the western Sudan.

Some of these early Yoruba may have helped to form the Bantu-speaking peoples in their homeland in the Cameroons. They may be the ancestors of the Luba of the southern Congo.

The Yoruba of West Africa settled in the forest region of the Lower Niger about A.D. 1000. There, among the other Negro communities, whose language they now came to use, they founded the kingdom of Ile-Ife.

Ile-Ife

Brass head, probably representing an early Oni of Ife, and thought to date from the 13th or 14th century

There are several legends of how this Yoruba state was founded. The most important tell of a founder chief called Oduduwa, who conquered the local inhabitants of Ile-Ife. His seven sons, says the legend, became the seven rulers of Yorubaland, who included the Alafin of Oyo and the Oba of Benin.

This is a story, but there is little doubt that the Yoruba at Ife did conquer the tribes round about, settle among them, and appoint new rulers. This happened during the three centuries from 1100 to 1400.

Ife, being the original town, was always looked upon by the Yoruba as their spiritual home. The Yoruba were gifted artists, and Ife became a centre for art and culture in this part of Africa. In recent years, several pieces of bronze sculpture and thousands of pieces of pottery have been unearthed near Ife. This craftwork was the result of two influences. First was the tradition of pottery manufacture among the local Negro peoples that had first flowered among the Nok community during the last centuries B.C. (see Chapter 9 of Book One). Second was the knowledge of brass-casting, developed on the Nile in the time of the Egyptian Empire. It may have been brought to West Africa by the ancestors of the Yoruba themselves.

The brass was cast by the 'lost-wax' method. Let us suppose that a head was to be made in brass. First, a model of the head was roughly prepared in clay. When this was dry, the head was covered by a coat of warm beeswax. The beeswax would of course cool and become hard. Then it was possible to scrape the details of the head on the surface of the wax. After that, the wax-covered model was again covered in clay, leaving a hole at the top and the bottom, and left to dry. Now the whole piece was baked hot. The wax ran out of the hole, leaving a space between the clay model and the clay covering. Into the hole at the top, molten brass was poured. When this had cooled hard, the outer layer of clay was broken away, leaving the brass model plain to see.

By 1300, brass-casting at Ife had reached a high standard, which was to some extent copied in other forest cities, notably Benin. When the Portuguese arrived two hundred years later, they were amazed at the quality of this craftsmanship. The bronzes of Ife are still among the finest pieces of sculpture in the world.

Oyo

Although Ife was the most cultured city in Yorubaland, Oyo was the most powerful.

Oyo was founded, says the legend, by Oranmiyan, a prince of Ife. The Edo people of Benin to the south-east were in trouble. They asked the Oni of Ife, whom they respected, to send a member of the Ife royal family to be their ruler. Oranmiyan was sent, but he did not like living among the Edo of Benin. After a short time he left and founded his own town at Oyo, about fifty miles north of Ife. This happened in about 1250.

Oyo was situated in the northern fringe of the forest, with more open grassland suitable for horses. In subsequent years the Alafin (ruler) of Oyo was able to develop a strong army, and by using cavalry—armed horsemen—he succeeded in repelling enemies such as the Nupe north of the Niger. He made his capital the centre for the trade that came southward to the forest belt from Hausaland in the north.

As a result, the Alafin of Oyo became the strongest ruler in Yorubaland. His power extended from the Niger in the north-east to Togoland in the west. To the south it was bounded by the region of the mangrove forest. Even Ife submitted to the rule of Oyo, although the people of Oyo still looked on the Oni of Ife as their spiritual leader.

The system of government in Oyo was remarkable. The Alafin was not all-powerful, and he had to show responsibility towards his people. He was chosen from among members of the royal family by a council of seven notables called the Oyo Mesi. If he used his power wrongly, he could be presented by the Basorun, leader of the Oyo Mesi, with an empty calabash which was a sign that he had to kill himself. 'The gods reject

Ivory pendant, probably representing an Oba of Benin

you, the people reject you, the earth rejects you,' he would be told.

Below the royal family, the palace officials and the Oyo Mesi were the army leaders. These were not hereditary, but were appointed by the Alafin. The Kakanfo, or army commander, was not allowed to lose a battle. If defeated, he had to take his own life. For this reason Oyo generals were usually successful. Some who suffered defeat went away to form new Yoruba communities elsewhere rather than return home.

The Alafin who began the expansion of the Oyo Empire, a successor of Oranmiyan, was a famous ruler named Shango. There is a story about him that he liked to use magic. One day, to show his power, he used it to call down lightning. The lightning struck his house and killed his wives and children. Stricken with grief, the king took his own life.

Though Oyo was not as large an empire as Mali and Songhai to the north, it grew to be a powerful state. Wars were fought against the Hausa Banza of Nupe across the river, and once the Yoruba were severely defeated. They were saved, however, by the leadership of a brilliant general, Ofonran, and the armies of Nupe were driven out. By 1600 the power of Oyo was at its greatest extent. Later, in the eighteenth century, even Dahomey was conquered and ruled for a short time.

The end of the Yoruba Empire

However, this large area, much of it in the rain forest with poor communications, was too large for the rulers of Oyo to govern properly. After about 1750, the empire began to break up. There were three reasons.

First, the more distant parts began to demand independence. In 1789 the King of Dahomey refused to pay tribute any more.

The second reason was the slave trade with the Europeans on the coast. This was increasing in the eighteenth century, and for this and other reasons the old trade with the north was declining. However, Oyo was too far north to gain much from the slave trade, and so became poorer and less important than other centres nearer the coast.

Thirdly, some of the leading subjects of the Alafin began to rebel against him. In a civil war which began in 1820, the Kakanfo Afonju, in particular, used the help of the Fulani, recent conquerors of the Hausa, to overthrow the Alafin Aole.

The Fulani then turned on Afonju, who was killed in battle,

and occupied Ilorin, a northern outpost of Oyo, and prevented the Yoruba from taking slaves from north of the Niger. The Yoruba had to have slaves to sell to the European traders, so they began to fight among themselves. Even Ife, the original home of the Yoruba, was now destroyed. In 1837 Oyo was moved south to a new site nearer the coast. Ibadan, however, between Oyo and Lagos, became the most important town.

Although the Yoruba, from their new centre in the forest, managed to keep the Fulani at bay, they were thus in a weak and divided condition when European traders and missionaries came inland in the late nineteenth century.

Benin

Meanwhile, to the south-east between the coast and the lower Niger, another kingdom had been flourishing, whose centre was the city of Benin.

The traditions of the Bini—that is, the Edo people of Benin— say that, like the Yoruba of Ife, their ancestors came long ago from the far-off Nile. The first dynasty at Benin, supposed to have been descended from the gods, was founded about A.D. 900. At this time the kings were called *Ogieso*, which means 'ruler of the sky'.

About 1160 the king, Osogau, was banished for misgovernment. For some years Benin was a republic. Eventually it was decided to return to monarchy, and Oduduwa, the Oni of Ife, was invited to send one of his sons to be ruler of Benin. Oranmiyan was sent.

Oranmiyan, as we have seen, did not want to continue living at Benin. Before he left, however, he married a princess of Benin, and their son now became the new Oba, with the title of Eweka I. This dynasty has continued to the present day.

The rulers of Benin, therefore, were now related to the rulers of Ife. For a long time they recognized this link. When the Oba of Benin died, the Oni of Ife would send his successor a sculptured brass head. However, another account says that he used to send a staff and a brass helmet. This was a sign that Benin was dependent on Ife, but by 1500 it had shaken off this dependence.

Brass-casting at Benin

About 1300 the wise Oba Oguola greatly admired the brass ornaments that were sent to him from Ife. Wanting to introduce the art to his own country, he asked for a craftsman to be

(left)
*Bronze plaque from Benin,
probably depicting
a Portuguese soldier*

(right)
*Bronze figure of a hunter
carrying an antelope*

sent. The man who came was Iguegha, a fine brass-smith who taught the people of Benin to cast brass by the lost-wax method.

The brass-smiths were strictly controlled by the Oba. The technique was kept secret. The craftsmen lived in a special street in the city called Igueroyo, after the name of the smith sent from Ife.

Before long the brasswork of Benin was as fine as that of Ife. It was greatly admired by the Portuguese when they visited the city after 1472.

Benin grows powerful through trade

When the Portuguese and other Europeans came to the coast after 1472, Benin began to grow wealthy. Lying midway between the Niger and Lagos—a coast town which the Edo of Benin claim to have founded—they were in a good position for trade. They bought European goods for themselves, and also for sale to the Yoruba inland. At this time guns and powder, and also fruits like pawpaws and coconuts, first entered the country. To the European traders the Edo exported pepper, ivory, palm-oil, cotton and—increasingly—slaves.

Being fairly near to the sea, Benin was visited by Portuguese, Dutch and English traders. From the accounts of these men

50

we know something of what Benin was like.

It was a large city surrounded by fortifications which extended for 28 miles. By the sixteenth century it had a population of several thousand. A high wall and a deep ditch surrounded the city, the entrances to which were guarded by strong wooden gates. A Dutch visitor in 1602 described thirty main streets, each a hundred and thirty feet wide. Houses were well-built with spacious verandas. Cooking was done inside the house, a hole in the roof permitting the smoke to escape. The Oba lived in a fine palace or *eguae* built between the two west walls of the city.

The city was kept clean, and well-established laws were enforced by the Oba's police. Life was not always easy or pleasant, however. Many slaves were kept, who were killed when their master died. Human sacrifices were carried out according to the rites of the pagan religion.

By 1650, Benin was at the height of its prosperity and power. A century later, however, its power and influence were gone.

The main reason for this decline was the slave trade (see Chapter 8). The Obas grew rich on this trade, and government went from bad to worse as they grew more corrupt. Wars—sometimes civil wars—were fought to gather slaves for sale.

The city of Benin in the 17th century, from a drawing (1668) by a Dutch geographer

The country round Benin became empty of people. Life became insecure, farming was ruined, and interest in art declined.

Meanwhile other states were having more success, and taking the trade from Benin. To the west, as we have seen, were the Yoruba. To the east, across the Niger, other tribes, notably the Ibo, were becoming powerful.

East of the Niger

While the Yoruba and Edo peoples, about whom we have been reading, had been settling west of the Niger, other Negro communities had crossed the Benue and settled east of the river, between the Benue, the Niger and the Cameroon Highlands.

The earliest of these settlers are believed to have been the Ijaw, who today live in and around the delta. They have a very old language. Probably they arrived about A.D. 1000 and became a river people, skilled at fishing and building canoes. Later they traded across the Niger with the city of Benin.

Another early group of settlers were the Ibibio. They lived farther east, between the Cross River and the Cameroons Mountain in the country known as Calabar. Later they traded with the Portuguese, who found the Cross River a useful inland waterway for their ships.

The Ijaw and the Ibibio had been pushed south by a strong tribe to the north of them—the Ibo. The Ibo were the most numerous of the people east of the Niger. Energetic and independent-minded, they did not like to have a strong chief or 'divine king' such as ruled in Oyo and Benin. Therefore they had no big capital city, but lived in small towns and villages all over Iboland. However, they believed in a supreme god, to whom they spoke through an oracle, 'Chukwu', who belonged to the Aro clan and became very important and wealthy, by selling advice about matters such as trade and war.

The Ibo, indeed, became great traders. They traded both with Benin across the Niger and, through the delta peoples, with the Europeans on the coast. Their main export was slaves. By 1600 they were growing fruits such as pineapple and pawpaw which had been brought to Africa by the Portuguese. By 1700 they were buying gunpowder, iron bars and cloth from African traders who came up from the coast. In exchange they sold slaves and rare woods. In the end they became the most numerous and powerful people in what was to become the eastern region of Nigeria.

7 Kingdoms of the Congo

To the east of the rain forests of the Niger delta stand the mountains and hills of the Cameroon Highlands. In this grassy hill country the Negroes of the west and the Hamites of the east had met and mingled in the centuries of Meroe and its decline. During the five centuries before and after the beginning of our era, the Bantu-speaking peoples had been formed.

Some of these energetic, iron-working people had, as we have seen, moved eastward to the Congo Highlands and the lake region of East Africa. Others moved south into the hills of Gabon between the Congo basin and the sea. A few moved into the forests of the Congo basin itself. There they found it easy, with their iron weapons, to drive out the Pygmies they found living there. Not many did this, however; it was difficult to grow food in the thick Congo forest.

In this chapter we shall follow the story of three African kingdoms that were formed in the more open country to the south of the Lower Congo—those of the Kongo, the Kuba and the Luba peoples. Here the forest opens out into grassland and plateau. From this plateau the southern tributaries of the Congo River come.

The kingdom of Kongo

Little is known of the early history of the Kongo before the Portuguese came. Arriving from the north, where they had made their way through the rain forest, by 1300 the Kongo were the strongest tribe between the Kwango River and the sea. Their capital was at Mbanza. This was about a hundred miles south of where Kinshasa is today.

Most tribes in the region were early Bantu settlers who were without chiefs. The Kongo, however, had a system of rule by chiefs. At first the ruler was not very powerful. A new chief was not always the eldest son, and he often had to fight for his rights against rival members of the royal family. However, by 1400 the power of the king was increasing; so too was the size of the kingdom. It extended to the Kwango River in the east and to the Bengo River, which flows into the Atlantic near Luanda, in the south. There were six provinces. Each was controlled by a strong governor, or sub-chief. Each governor sent a tribute of raffia and cowrie shells to the king every year.

Kingdoms of the Congo basin 1300–1600

The king, or Mani-Kongo, also received tribute from some of the tribes to the north of the river.

Raffia is a fibre made from palm leaves. The Kongo were skilful at weaving it into cloth and mats with ornate patterns. This weaving was greatly admired by the Portuguese when they first came to the country. Cowrie shells were obtained from the sea, especially from near Luanda. They were used as money in this part of Africa, as also, in Book One, we found them being used by the Arabs on the east coast. The Kongo did not know about gold, and when the Portuguese came and offered gold presents, the Africans refused them, demanding cowrie shells instead.

Although the Kongo had no knowledge of gold, they knew how to make copper and, of course, iron. There was iron in the hill country around Mbanza, and this was what made the Kongo into a more powerful tribe than their neighbours. With iron hoes they cultivated millet and sorghum. Fruits grew abundantly in the forest. There were no cattle here, but meat was obtained by hunting.

The ruins of Sao Salvador

Congo forest

Portuguese influence

It was at this time, when the Kongo kingdom was becoming an organized state, that Portuguese sailors in 1482 reached the mouth of the Congo River. Diego Cao, the Portuguese captain, was impressed with the size and power of the Kongo state. He persuaded the King of Portugal to make an alliance with the Mani-Congo Nzinga Nkuwu, who accepted missionaries and teachers. Nzinga's son was baptized and later became King

Afonso I. A church was built at Mbanza, which was renamed Sao Salvador.

All this, however, did the Kongo more harm than good. Kongo chiefs became jealous of Portuguese influence and rebelled against the king. In 1526 Afonso appealed to Portugal for help, but none came, because Portugal now had many other trading posts to think about, especially in India and the Far East. The Portuguese planters on Sao Thomé Island began to buy slaves in Kongo country for work on their plantations. The Kongo government tried to stop this but were unable to do so, because the chiefs wanted Portuguese cloth and guns so badly that they were prepared to capture people and sell them as slaves in order to obtain these articles.

By 1600 the Kongo state had split up into parts which were frequently at war with one another.

Angola

The story was much the same in the highlands of Angola, farther south. There the strongest tribe was the Mbundu, who had arrived from the west and made themselves powerful over earlier Bantu settlers, just as the Kongo had done to the north of them.

The ruler of the Mbundu had the title of Ngola, which is why the Portuguese gave this name to the country. The Portuguese were sure there were silver mines in Mbundu country. There were even stories that silver grew on the trees. Finding none, the Portuguese took slaves instead. The Mbundu therefore retreated inland to Matamba. They fought repeatedly against the invaders under leaders of whom the heroic Queen Nzinga (c. 1580–1663) is the best known.

The Portuguese kept control of the Angola coast and of their trading posts like Luanda and Lobito. The Mbundu and other tribes kept their independence till the nineteenth century. But wars and slave trading had once again weakened the authority of rulers, and stopped the growth of an organized African state.

The Kuba

Foreign influence could not, however, damage the growth of two important kingdoms far inland. The first of these belonged to the Kuba tribe in the southern Congo, who built a powerful state east of the Kwango River, among the tributaries of the Kasai.

At first the Kuba had lived in Gabon, north of the Congo

The 17th century church of Nazare in Luanda, Angola

River. When the Portuguese arrived and began to trade for slaves after 1500, the Kuba left their villages and travelled inland. They crossed the great river in canoes and settled on its south bank, living by fishing and hunting.

One hundred years later a wandering tribe of brigands, the Jaga, came marauding from the south-east, and drove out the Kuba. The Kuba took to their canoes, and escaped up the Kasai River. Finally they settled in more open country between the Kasai and Sankuru Rivers.

When they arrived there, the Kuba were still a small tribe of hunters and fishermen. From the Gabon they brought the knowledge of copper and iron working. Among the people of their new country they now learnt to cultivate millet. They did not weave raffia as the Kongo did, but made their clothes from bark cloth.

The Bushongo lead the Kuba

A leading Kuba tribe was the Bushongo clan. During their migration up the Kasai, they had appointed a 'captain of canoes'. Upon arrival in the new country, this man continued to act as chief of the clan. He must have been a capable leader, for when he died the Bushongo headmen elected one of his sons to succeed him. At first the system of election was customary, and an unpopular chief could be deposed. Before long, however, the position of chief became hereditary.

Now the Bushongo invented new ceremonial, and treated their kings with growing respect. Each local chief had to take an oath of allegiance at the beginning of a reign, and was obliged to present the new king with a wife as a token of his loyalty. Councils of elders were appointed among the subject tribes, and ministers controlled different departments of government. Tribute was paid annually. In fact, a powerful new state was growing along the Upper Kasai.

Shyama Ngoongo

Other Kuba tribes, however, were jealous of the power wielded by the Bushongo. Some time about 1750, a revolution occurred. The Bushongo king was killed, and his place was taken by a Kuba adventurer from the west named Shyama Ngoongo.

Shyama had lived on the Kwango River, and knew the customs of the Bakongo and other tribes in the west. Despite his adventurous career, he now proved himself one of the steadiest and wisest of African kings. To the Kuba he brought craftsmen who taught them how to weave raffia, and also the art of woodcarving. This art became highly developed, so that Kuba woodcarving is among the finest in Africa. Shyama also taught his people how to grow maize, groundnuts and tomatoes, crops which the Portuguese had brought to Africa from Brazil. Trade increased. The Kuba traded with the Portuguese on the west coast, and with the Bantu of the Congo Highlands in the east. They were becoming peaceful, wealthy and powerful.

Kuba power was exercised wisely. Subject tribes were allowed to govern themselves, provided they paid the annual tribute taxes. Shyama, however, made sure of his strength by making his capital into a large town. There the young men were trained to serve in a standing army.

Shyama, the wise king, was regarded with great reverence by the Kuba people. Legends grew up that his ancestors were descended from the gods. Other African tribes of the southern Congo, such as the Luyi and the Bemba, have legends like this. They were in fact inventing a kind of 'divine kingship'. It is interesting that this happened because these Bantu states were a long way from the Sudanic kingdoms in the north.

The Luba

Meanwhile a third great Congo kingdom had been growing up still farther east, on the northern part of the plateau which today we call Katanga. This was the Luba Empire.

We are not sure where the Luba came from. Because of the name (Luba=Ruba), some people have thought they were connected with the early Yoruba long ago. Certainly we know that they came from the north, perhaps moving up the valley of the Upper Congo River, or possibly along tributaries of the Kasai.

By 1300 there was a Luba kingdom on the Upper Lualaba River. A burial ground of that date has been found along some miles of river bank on the Upper Lualaba near Lake Kisale. In the graves have been found copper goods, and among them some H-shaped copper bars such as the Luba are known to have made.

Luba traditions say that this early kingdom was ruled by chiefs of the Songye clan, a strong tribe to the north. In about 1500, however, there was a revolt. The Luba drove out their Songye rulers and set up a new Luba Empire. It extended from Lake Tanganyika to the Upper Kasai.

To the south of this Luba Empire lay the region of present-day Katanga. Here lived the Lunda tribe. In about 1600 a Luba prince called Ilunga made a marriage alliance with the Lunda Queen, Lueji. Their descendants, the Lunda emperors, were independent of the Luba. They were known by the title of *Mwata Yamvo*, which means 'Lord of Wealth'. This wealth lay in ivory and copper which were both in abundant supply, and which the Mwata Yamvos traded to the Portuguese in the west and later to the Arabs in the east. They also traded, as we have seen (see Chapter 12, Book One), with Monomotapa's kingdom south of the Zambezi.

We shall read more about this Lunda Empire in Chapter 11.

8 New trade comes to West Africa

In the last two chapters, mention has several times been made of the Portuguese. This is natural, because after 1480 the Portuguese had a considerable effect on the inhabitants of the West African coast, and of the Congo basin and Angola. In the next two chapters we turn to look more closely at the arrival of the Portuguese and of other European traders.

We shall begin by taking a look at the inhabitants of the west coast at that time. The Empires of Mali and Songhai, described in previous chapters, had flourished along the Niger River. The kingdoms of the Asante and of Dahomey and Oyo had been centred on the northern fringe of the rain forest. Of the largest West African states, only Benin had extended its power as far as the sea.

Map to illustrate the early European trade on the West African coast 1500–1800

In the coastal forest belt between Cape Verde and the Niger delta lived Negro peoples. These Negroes, as we saw in Chapter 8, Book One, had slowly been driven south and west by stronger tribes from the north ever since 5000 B.C. Most of them occupied their present homes long before the beginning of our era.

By A.D. 1400 most of these west coast African tribes knew how to smelt iron. Several had discovered the value of ivory and of gold which they exported to the empires of the Niger. Some of this gold, as we have seen, found its way across the Sahara to the Berbers in the north, and to Europe.

The west coast

Let us look more closely at the west coast as far as the Bight of Benin. It can be divided into four parts. First is the stretch around Cape Verde, including the Senegal and Gambia Rivers. We call this region Senegambia. Inland were the peoples of Tekrur, whom we have already met. The strongest coast tribes were the Jalofo and the Kantora.

South of Senegambia is the coast between the mountains of Sierra Leone and Cape Palmas. Inland here lived the Sosso, who had taken refuge in the hills after Sundiata of Mali had driven them away from the Upper Niger in 1240. Along the coast lived the Bullom and the Temne peoples, who had arrived there long before.

East of Cape Palmas lies the third stretch of coast, centred on the Volta River. Because of the rich gold trade which developed here later, this came to be known to Europeans as the Gold Coast. Inland, in the hill country to the west of the Volta, lived the Asante tribe. These were members of the Akan group of peoples who, as we have seen, came down from the north about 1100. Along the coast lived a number of tribes, of whom the strongest were the Nzima and the Fante (both related to the Akan group), the Ga and the Ewe. Many of these coast people were keen fishermen. They also traded sometimes with the Asante and tribes inland.

Farther east still is the fourth part of the coast, from the Bight of Benin to the Niger delta. From here the European traders obtained the biggest supply of slaves, so that it came to be known as the Slave Coast. Inland were the strong states of Togo, Dahomey, Oyo and Benin. Yoruba and Edo peoples also dominated the sea coast.

The coast peoples

The tribes along the coast were many. We have only given the names of a few. They had different ways of life. Some, like the Asante and the Ga, had strong chiefs. Others had no proper chiefs at all, and just lived in groups of huts under headmen.

There was no unity among these tribes, and they spoke different languages. They continued to respect the forest gods because the Moslem missionaries seldom tried to settle in the unhealthy forest belt. Some Moslems were working along the Gambia River by 1400, but that was all. Thus there was no learning along the coast. Except for a small amount of trade inland, the coast peoples were isolated.

Then, in the fifteenth century, a change came from an unexpected direction—the sea.

The Portuguese

Prince Henry the Navigator

One morning in 1445 the people of Cape Verde were astounded to see a strange ship, a caravel, with two masts and triangular sails, lying off the shore. From it came a small boat, rowed by men with long dark hair and light skins. Stepping ashore, the leader persuaded the watching Africans to take him to the local chief's village.

There the stranger introduced himself as Nuna Tristao. He came from Portugal, and had been sent by Prince Henry, a son of the king.

Henry the Navigator, as the prince was called, had heard of West African gold from the Berbers of the Mahgrib. He thought it might be possible to trade with West Africa by sea, instead of by crossing the desert as the Berbers had always done. After founding a sailing school at Sagres in Portugal in 1419, Prince Henry had sent ship after ship to try and find the way round the Guinea coast—*Guinea* was the Portuguese word for 'land of the black people'. Nuna Tristao was one of the prince's captains.

After Nuna had explained all this to the people of Cape Verde, he made a treaty of friendship with them and sailed home. Three years later he returned and sailed as far as the Rio Grande, fifty miles south of the Gambia, but there the people were not so friendly, and he was killed as he came ashore.

Diego Gomes

Meanwhile Prince Henry was sending out more caravels. In 1458 Diego Gomes sailed along the Gambia River as far as

A Portuguese caravel,
from a 16th century drawing

Kantora. The people there told Diego of rich gold-mines farther up-river, but he decided it was safer to return. His voyage was not wasted, for he obtained 180 lb of gold from an African chief on the north bank, and a gift of ivory and slaves from the Jalofo. Another chief, Numimansa, asked for a Christian missionary to be sent, and next year Prince Henry sent an abbot, who built a little church at Juffure. This was the first Christian church in tropical Africa.

Prince Henry died in 1460. His life's work had seen the beginning of European activity in West Africa, including trade in gold and ivory, missionary work and slave trading.

Further voyages

The Portuguese, encouraged by their king, continued to explore the west coast. In 1462 Pedro da Sintra made a map of the coast of Sierra Leone. Nine years later, two captains sent by Fernao Gomes discovered the mouth of the Sao Jaoa River (or Pra River). Fernao Gomes had been given the monopoly of the Gold Coast trade for five years, but after that the Portuguese government took direct control. In 1481, resolving to profit from the rich gold in the area, the Portuguese built Elmina Castle twenty miles farther east of the river mouth.

The following year, in 1482, Diego Cao sailed right along the coast, and south as far as the mouth of the Congo River. By this time the Portuguese were hoping to find a sea route round Africa to India. Stories that this would be possible had

Sierra Leone coastline today

come to them from Pedro Covilhao, a traveller in Ethiopia. In the next chapter we shall read how they succeeded in doing this.

Meanwhile Portuguese caravels were coming, sometimes singly, sometimes two or three at a time, to the Guinea Coast every year. Many trading posts were set up, and plantations were also begun on the islands of Sao Thomé and Fernando Po.

Other countries send ships

Other European countries soon heard of the Portuguese success. At first, Spanish ships started to come for slaves; but in 1480, by the Treaty of Tordesillas, the King of Spain recognized the Portuguese monopoly in West Africa.

Instead, the Portuguese soon had to face competition from the French and the English. In 1492 a French ship captured a Portuguese vessel laden with gold bound from Elmina to Lisbon. Such fights were frequent. Forts like Elmina, in fact, were built less for protection against Africans than for defence against foreign ships. Between 1500 and 1600, French and English 'sea-dogs' captured many Portuguese ships and took their gold.

The fortress of Elmina as seen from the lagoon

By this time the Portuguese were also busy in Brazil, and in Mozambique, about which we shall read in the next chapter, and in India. They began to lose their hold on the Guinea Coast of Africa. By 1600 the French had their own trading stations north of the Gambia. The English had stations on the river itself, and two English trading companies sent ships regularly to the west coast. After 1600, Dutch sailors also joined in. The Dutch captured Elmina Castle from the Portuguese in 1637.

Trading companies

After the Portuguese, the Europeans who set up forts and trading posts were not sent by their governments, but by trading companies. These companies were of course encouraged by their governments, who took part of the profit. In 1561, for

Christiansborg Castle under the British flag

example, the 'Company of Merchant Adventurers for Guinea' was formed in London. Other companies followed. The most famous of all was the 'Royal Adventurers of England Trading into Africa', formed in 1660. In the same way the French, the Dutch, the Danes and the Swedes all had trading companies.

All these companies built forts, which were abandoned, sold, attacked, captured or exchanged from time to time. Some were strong castles like Elmina, Cape Coast and Christiansborg in present-day Ghana. Others were quite small and had only one or two Europeans to defend them.

A company which built a trading post or a fort paid rent for it to the local African chief. The rent for Elmina Castle was two ounces of gold a month. Cape Coast paid four ounces a month. The Europeans did not claim land or try to rule the Africans until after 1880.

The Europeans did not often travel inland; instead the Africans came to the coast to trade with them. The chief reason for this was malaria, a disease the Europeans did not understand, but which killed many. They did, however, sail up the Senegal and Gambia Rivers, which were deep enough for their ships.

The slave trade

Quite soon after they began coming to West Africa the European traders found that gold and ivory and other African goods did not by themselves make enough profit. Therefore they began to take slaves as well. The Portuguese, as we have seen, took slaves from the Jalofo of Gambia as early as 1458, though this was a gift. Soon more were being taken in exchange for money or goods.

In the next century, plantations and mines were started in the West Indies, Brazil and Central America. Because the climate in those places was too hot and humid for Europeans to work in, many more slaves were now needed.

John Hawkins, an Englishman, was one of the first big slave traders. In 1562 he made his first slave trading voyage. He took Africans to the West Indies and Spanish America, where he sold them for hides, sugar and silver. These he took and sold in England. He became a rich man.

The Portuguese, however, were the main slave traders in the sixteenth century. Between 1530 and 1560 they carried 900,000 slaves across the Atlantic. But the other trading companies joined in. Altogether between 1500 and 1864 about twenty million Africans were taken from West Africa to the New World. That is why there are so many people of African descent in South America, the West Indies and the United States of America today.

It is true that the Africans had slaves in their own communities, but they were usually well treated as members of the family. Sometimes they were sold to the Berber traders across the Sahara. Even this was different from being captured, sold, taken on a terrible sea voyage, and often harshly treated in a strange land from which there was no return.

African chiefs took a leading part in the trade. The King of Dahomey was one of the greatest slave traders, and Europeans used to come to his town to do business with him. Farther west, on the other hand, along the Gold Coast, African traders acting as middlemen obtained slaves inland and brought them down to the coast for the European traders to buy.

Effects of this early foreign trade

Trade is usually good for mankind: it makes possible the exchange of ideas as well as of goods, so it causes civilization to spread. Wealth is increased, and with it opportunities for leisure and education.

Early European trade in West Africa did not have this effect. West Coast peoples had always been poor, and had sometimes fought one another for land or food. Wars now became more frequent, but wealth did not increase. Europeans used the help of African chiefs in fighting other Africans or against other companies. Guns came to be commonly used.

It was worse in the interior. Strong tribes like the Asante became stronger and raided other tribes for slaves. Formerly the chief had been the voice and servant of the people. Now chiefs became powerful despots like the King of Dahomey. European goods did little to improve African life. On the other hand the loss of young men and women ruined the villages.

Few missionaries came to teach the people. The Portuguese, it is true, sent missionaries in the sixteenth century to the Kongo, and also to Monomotapa in Mashonaland. In each of these states there were some Christian rulers for a time. However, the mission work was spoilt by the ambition of traders and not supported enough from Europe. Portugal became too interested in her colonies in the Far East and gave up many of her African trading posts. On the West African coast, except for the Gambia and Senegal settlements, there was no missionary work at all.

Not until the slave trade ended in the nineteenth century did West Africa begin to benefit from European trade. This was to begin in the oil palm region of the Niger delta.

The West Coast slave trade

An African protest

Moreover, Sir, in our kingdoms there is another great inconvenience which is of little service to God, and this is that many of our people, keenly desirous as they are of the wares and things of your kingdoms, which are brought here by your people, and in order to satisfy their voracious appetite, seize many of our people, freed and exempt men; and very often it happens that they kidnap even noblemen and the sons of noblemen, and take them to be sold to the white men who are in our kingdom. And as soon as they are taken by the white men they are immediately ironed and branded with fire.

That is why we beg of Your Highness to help and assist us in this matter, commanding your traders that they should not send here either merchants or wares, because it is our will that in these kingdoms there should not be any trade of slaves nor outlet for them.

Letters from King Affonso of Kongo to the King of Portugal, 1526

A European account

I remember that in the year 1681 an English trader got three hundred good slaves almost for nothing besides the trouble of receiving them at the beach in his boats, as the local men brought them from the field of battle, having obtained a victory over a neighbouring nation, and taken a great number of prisoners.

At other times slaves are so scarce there, that in 1682 I could get but eight from one end of the coast to the other, not only because we were a great number of trading ships on the coast at the same time, but by reason the natives were everywhere at peace . . .

As to the different sorts of goods the Europeans generally carry thither for trade; each nation commonly supplies the coast with such goods as their respective countries can afford; and what they want at home for well assorting their cargo, they buy in other parts of Europe.

Jean Barbot, a French trader

9 Merchant sailors on the east coast

The statue of Bartolomeo Dias in Cape Town

Meanwhile, the Portuguese had been trying to find their way round the southern cape to India. It was known that they would be able to buy spices there, which were nearly as valuable as the gold they were seeking in West Africa. These spices were ginger, cinnamon, pepper and nutmeg, which improved the taste of food. In Europe people killed their cattle at the end of the summer and kept the meat salted all through the winter. To improve the flavour of the meat, rich people paid a lot of money for spices.

Formerly traders had gone from Europe to India by land. Later, however, the Ottoman Turks had built a new Moslem Empire that stretched from North Africa to Persia. Christian traders were not allowed to pass through. The Portuguese, however, believed they could reach India by sea.

In 1487 Bartolomeo Dias sailed past the Cape of Good Hope, but his men were frightened by violent storms, and he had to turn back. Ten years later, however, Vasco da Gama, another Portuguese captain, tried again with three ships. This time the Portuguese continued round the Cape and then east and north along the coast.

The Portuguese reach Mozambique

One day in March 1498 the Swahili of Mozambique were going about their morning business when a shout was heard. A man came running up from the harbour to warn the guards that three strange ships were approaching from beyond the reef. They carried more sails than Arab dhows, so the Swahili thought they must be Turkish ships. When the ships reached the harbour the visitors were welcomed and given food.

Soon, however, it was discovered that the strangers were Christians from Portugal. The Moslems of Mozambique knew that the Kalifs had been fighting wars against the Christians of Europe for a long time. The people of Mozambique therefore drove the Portuguese away.

Vasco da Gama was both surprised to find such a large town on the African coast and disappointed to be treated in this way. His voyage round the Cape had taken six months. He needed fresh food and water, and also hoped to find a pilot to show him the way across the sea to India.

Mombasa from the anchorage a hundred years ago

They reach Mombasa and Malindi

Vasco da Gama

The Portuguese therefore sailed away northward along the coast. They did not stop at Kilwa, but they could see it in the distance and were again amazed at the appearance of a large town with mosques and streets and many houses. A similar view awaited them at Mombasa, and here they decided to land.

In the meantime, however, some Swahili sailed in a fast dhow from Mozambique to tell the people of Mombasa that the strangers were Christians, and that there had been a fight. When the Sultan of Mombasa heard this, he planned to trick Vasco da Gama by being friendly. When the ships had entered the harbour, he would sink them and kill the Portuguese.

Vasco da Gama waited outside the harbour, feeling suspicious of the Arabs. They brought him presents, but he still would not enter the harbour. Next day some Swahili came in boats and tried to cut the ropes holding the ships to anchor. The Portuguese captured two of them, and made them tell of the Sultan's plans. The news made Vasco da Gama decide not to find a pilot in Mombasa. He sailed on to Malindi instead.

The people of Malindi were rivals of the people of Mombasa. The Portuguese had discovered this, and thought the Sultan of Malindi would help them. They soon found they were right. The Sultan sent a present of six sheep, and promised to find a pilot. From that time the Portuguese and the people of Malindi were friends and allies.

The Portuguese in India

With the April monsoon wind blowing hard on their sails, the Portuguese crossed the sea to India, and came to Calicut.

The ruler of Calicut was very rich—much richer than the Portuguese. He even laughed at the presents Vasco da Gama had brought, but the Portuguese captain promised to come again with better presents. The Indians gave him spices of all kinds, together with silk from China, cotton cloth from India, and precious stones from Burma and Ceylon.

Then Vasco da Gama and his ships sailed for home: they had been away for three years. The King of Portugal and all the people gave them a great welcome. The king listened with great interest to all the stories they had to tell. He was amazed to hear about all the rich towns along the east coast of Africa.

The Portuguese seize East Africa

After this, the Portuguese sent ships year after year to India. They built forts at Ormuz in the Persian Gulf, at Goa in India, and at places in the East Indies. Portugal became wealthy and strong.

To make the journey safely, the Portuguese ships had to stop on the East African coast. They needed to mend the sails, and to take in fresh water and vegetables for the crew. But many Arab towns disliked the Portuguese and refused to help them. Of course, the Arabs were Moslem and the Portuguese were Christian, but the main reason was that the Arabs wanted the trade in the Indian Ocean all for themselves. Being determined to take this trade away from them, the Portuguese decided to conquer the East African towns.

Between 1502 and 1507, the Portuguese captured most of the towns. They were able to do this because they were determined fighters, and because they had better guns than the Arabs.

First, the Portuguese went to Kilwa and told the Sultan to pay tribute. He refused, so the Portuguese sent soldiers into the town and occupied it. Later they built Kilwa Castle, which is still standing today. After occupying Kilwa, they attacked Mombasa. This was more difficult. There was a hard fight in the narrow streets and on the rooftops. In the end the Portuguese won, after many houses had been destroyed.

In the north, the Portuguese made Malindi their chief town. The Sultan of Malindi was a friend, and did not have to pay tribute like other sultans. Later a fort was built at Mombasa,

*Memorial pillar erected to
Vasco da Gama at Malindi:
an early 19th century drawing*

and the Portuguese officer at Malindi was called 'Captain of
the coast of Malindi and the Fort of Mombasa'. Farther north
still the Portuguese visited Ethiopia, and in 1540 they helped
the Christian king of Ethiopia to defeat the Moslem invaders
(see Chapter 11, Book One).

In the south, the chief town of the Portuguese was at Mozambique. There too the Sultan was friendly. The Portuguese built
a fort and a hospital, and the church of St Gabriel. All these
were built of stone. Around the town the Portuguese planted
fruit trees and vegetable gardens, so that sailors on their way
to India could have fresh food. In this way, new crops and
fruits, such as maize, groundnuts and pawpaw, came to East
Africa.

The Captain at Mozambique controlled Sofala and the gold
trade, which the Portuguese were now taking from the Arabs.

The Portuguese in Mashonaland

As we know, the Portuguese had come to East Africa because it was on the way to India and the spice trade.

Soon after their arrival, however, they heard about the gold trade at Sofala (see Chapters 12 and 13, Book One). Gold was even more valuable than spices. Adventurers from Spain, a country next to Portugal, were discovering gold in South America. The Portuguese had found some in West Africa, but not enough. If they could find gold in East Africa they would be as rich and powerful as Spain, their great rival.

The Portuguese decided to find out where the gold at Sofala came from. In 1512, Antonio Fernandes with some African porters was sent into Mashonaland through the Sabi valley. Fernandes was an educated man who had offended the King of Portugal. To win a pardon, he had to perform some dangerous service. This journey was that service.

Fernandes reached Monomotapa's capital at Fura Mountain, and was given a friendly greeting by the Shona. On his return he reported that there was much gold, especially in Manicaland. The people were digging for it, sometimes fifty feet deep under the ground. In other places gold was washed from the streams. Nuggets as big as a man's fingernail were to be found. The climate, according to Fernandes, was good for Europeans to live in.

Gonzales da Silveira

Many years passed. The Portuguese were busy winning the coast from the Arabs as far north as Malindi.

At last in 1561 a Jesuit missionary arrived in Mashonaland. He was Gonzales da Silveira, and he had come from Goa in India. He had heard of Monomotapa and wanted to convert him to Christianity.

The Monomotapa at this time was Nogoma Mapunzagatu, a young boy who was still being helped by his mother. He welcomed da Silveira with gifts of gold, cattle and slaves, but the priest declined them, saying he only wanted to win the hearts and minds of the people. At once he began teaching and baptizing.

The Arabs at Fura Mountain were angry. They feared that the Portuguese would now come and take all their trade. They told Nogoma that Silveira was using bad magic in order to destroy the kingdom. The young king was frightened, and decided to kill the missionary. Silveira was strangled in the night, and his body was thrown into the river, together with the bodies of several newly-baptized people.

When this news reached Portugal, more missionaries were sent. They continued working in Mashonaland for a hundred years, but their influence disappeared when the Portuguese were finally driven away.

Trade in Mashonaland

The first Portuguese trading expedition came to Mashonaland in 1569. This time, in spite of the Arabs, Monomotapa agreed that the Europeans could dig for gold and silver, or buy it from the Africans, in certain places. In return, they had to pay a tax in cloth, and also help Monomotapa in war against enemy tribes.

The Portuguese now built trading posts at Masapa on the Upper Mazoe River and at two other places. All their trade going into and out of the country had to pass through these posts. True to their promise, they helped Monomotapa Gatsi Rusere (1596–1627) in his wars. After this, a new treaty was made, by which the white men were allowed to sit in the presence of the king, and did not have to bow low and clap their hands.

The Shona drive out the Portuguese

The Shona, however, resented the growing influence of the Portuguese. In 1629 Monomotapa Kapararidze joined with the Arabs and made war on the white men. A great battle at Fura Mountain was won by the Portuguese and their allies. Kapararidze was killed and his place was taken by Mavura, a nephew, who had Portuguese support.

For a time all was peaceful again, and trade revived. However, the Arabs continued to make trouble, and the Portuguese were always insecure. Finally, in 1693, the Shona made another great effort. We have read in Chapter 12, Book One, how Monomotapa made an alliance with Changamire in the south, and how the Portuguese were finally driven from the country.

This was really a disaster for the Shona as well as for the Portuguese, because it meant less trade. There was no hope of a Portuguese revival, however, for they were also struggling without success against other enemies on the coast. The most important of these were the Arabs.

The Portuguese at Mombasa

From the beginning, the Arabs had hated the Portuguese for taking away their trade, and for winning control of the Indian Ocean. The people of Mombasa especially made trouble. In 1588 the Turks were fighting a war against Portugal and Spain in the Mediterranean. They heard of the quarrel between Mombasa and the Portuguese, and sent a fleet to help the people of Mombasa. A rebellion started.

Ships and soldiers were sent from Goa to punish the people of Mombasa and to defeat the Turks. This might have been difficult, because the Turks were brave fighters with good weapons. But just at this time a fierce group of Bantu warriors called waZimba appeared on the mainland. The Zimba were not a proper tribe and we do not know where they came from. They were terrible savages and used to eat the flesh of their victims.

The Zimba rushed across the shallow water to the island of Mombasa, and killed everyone they could find. Many Arabs, Swahili and Turks were killed, as well as some Portuguese. After feasting and dancing, the Zimba left Mombasa, and the Portuguese who had come from Goa occupied it again.

After leaving Mombasa, some of the Zimba went north to Malindi, but there they were defeated by a brave Bantu tribe called waSegeju. Many Zimba were killed. The rest of the Zimba retreated southward, slaughtering people wherever they went. When they came to the Zambezi valley, they attacked and killed the Africans and Portuguese there. After that, the Zimba passed on and disappeared.

Fort Jesus

At Mombasa, the Portuguese then built a great stone fort which they called Fort Jesus. It was started in 1592. It had high walls and a great courtyard inside. At each corner was a tower from which defenders could fire at attackers. Around the outside a deep ditch was dug. The front of the fort looked out over the sea.

For a hundred years, Portuguese soldiers lived in the fort with their wives and families. They put down rebellions in Mombasa, and kept the Portuguese strong in other parts of the coast.

During this time, from about 1600 to 1700, the enemies of Portugal grew stronger. Other countries in Europe fought against Portugal, and started to send ships to India. The Arabs in Arabia saw this happen, and began to fight to win back the East African towns. In the interior the Bantu tribes and the

Fort Jesus, built by the Portuguese in 1593

Nilo-Hamites were increasing in numbers, and kept making war on the Portuguese.

At last even Fort Jesus was not strong enough to protect them.

Omani Arabs

There was a great ruler of Oman in Arabia, whose name was Seif bin Sultan. In 1696 he sent seven ships to attack Mombasa. The town was captured, and the Arabs besieged Fort Jesus.

In the fort were about two thousand five hundred people, of whom about a hundred were Portuguese. Months passed, and there was not enough food for so many. Then there came a terrible sickness, and hundreds died. After nearly three years, there were only twenty people left alive in the fort. They surrendered to the Arabs.

This was the end of Portuguese rule on the north part of the coast. Without Fort Jesus they could not control the other towns. The new rulers from Oman often treated the people very badly. Sometimes the Portuguese were asked for help, but they were not strong enough. They were only able to hold on to Mozambique, and their trading posts in the Zambezi valley.

In the next chapter we shall read more of what had been happening in the interior of East Africa, and how east coast trade was just beginning to affect the lives of people inland.

El Masoudi, the Arabian traveller, had reported that black-skinned people—'the people of Zanj'— were living on the east coast by the time of his visit in 916. These people were the first wave of Bantu-speaking settlers who had arrived in that part of Africa during the previous two or three centuries. They must have been the ancestors of coast tribes such as the Taita and the Nyika in Kenya, the Shambaa and the Zaramo along the Zanzibar coast, and the Ngindo and the Makwa farther south towards the Rovuma River. During the next few hundred years, more Bantu-speaking people continued to find their way to East Africa from the region of the Congo Highlands.

Now we come to a new series of movements. These are very important, and to understand them you must look carefully at the map. They begin with an event in the north-east about A.D. 1300.

The Galla

Some time about 1300, a new Hamitic people arrived in Somaliland from South Arabia. These were the Galla. They were a tall, brown-skinned, straight-nosed people who herded cattle. They had the custom of age-sets, which meant that all boys born in the same year grew up together, trained together, and fought together in war. This custom later spread to many of the Bantu tribes of Kenya.

First, the Galla went south-west to the country which is now north-east Kenya. Then they moved north. By about 1450 they were north of Lake Rudolf. During their migration, they met some early Hamites and Stone Age hunters; but these were few and there was room for the Galla. It was not until the Galla met the Sidama Hamites north of Lake Rudolf that they stopped.

The Galla and the Sidama were both cattle-keeping Hamitic tribes, but they were fighting tribes and there were wars between them for grazing lands. Many Sidama Hamites were pushed out of their homes to the west, towards the Upper Nile.

Hima and Tutsi

After reaching the Nile, some of these Sidama moved south with their long-horned cattle, through the lake region, till they came to Ruanda and Burundi north of Lake Tanganyika. Here

The spread of chieftainship from the lake region to East Africa about 1700–1800

Map labels:

NILOTES
LWO
NILO-HAMITES
L. Rudolf
GALLA
HAMITES
LWO
NYORO
GANDA
Mt. Kenya △
KIKUYU
SOMALI
Here there were strong chiefs
L. Nyanza
KAMBA
Here there were no chiefs
B A N T U
SUKUMA
MASAI
TAITA
Mt. Kilimanjaro △
NYIKA
NYAMWEZI
MASAI
CHAGA
SHAMBAA
L. Tanganyika
GOGO
INDIAN OCEAN
LUBA
Here there were strong chiefs
L. Rukwa
HEHE
KINGA
Livingstone Mts.
BISA
BEMBA
L. Malawi

Legend:

KIKUYU — Tribes without chiefs They came earlier

→ Spread of tribes with NTEMI chieftainship

⇒ Spread of tribes with other chieftainship

Nilo-Hamites who had come after 1500

0   100   200   300
Miles

they conquered the Bantu, who were Iru and Hutu. The traditions of these Bantu tell of how they were conquered long ago by a tall and able people, a race of heroes whom they called the Chwezi. We believe that these people were the Sidama from the north. Their descendants today are called Hima in the north, that is, in southern Uganda and Ruanda, and are known as Tutsi in the south, that is, in Burundi.

The Chwezi chiefs did not mix very much with the early Bantu, but kept to themselves the special task of ruling. This separation of the ruling class in Ruanda-Burundi has continued until recent times. They became strong and able rulers. However, at this time, if not before, they became a Bantu-speaking people.

Many of the customs of Uganda and Ruanda-Burundi have come from the Chwezi, the ancestors of the Hima and Tutsi. Much ceremonial attended the life of the chief, or king. These kings lived in large palaces built in a cone-shape, rather like the palace in which the Kabaka of Bugunda lived until the revolution of 1966. Wooden drinking vessels now came to be used, an old Sidama custom. The Chwezi taught their subjects how to make bark cloth, how to cultivate coffee, and how to dig wells through rock, using iron picks. They brought in new kinds of spear and shield.

The Chwezi ruled most of the lake region in peace for about two hundred years until the Lwo invasion of about 1600, about which we shall read later in this chapter.

Nilo-Hamites: the Masai

Meanwhile, others of the Sidama Hamites, who were pushed out of their homes by the Galla and went towards the Nile, mixed with the Nilotic peoples who lived there. In this way, they formed a new people whom we call the *Nilo-Hamites*. This change happened about 1400–1450.

A hundred years later, these Nilo-Hamites were moving southward, along Lake Rudolf and into the great Rift Valley. Later they split into two main tribes, the Masai and the Nandi. You will read mostly about the Masai. Other tribes were the Turkana and the Suk.

The Masai, like the Sidama, had come from a very dry country. For many months there was little grass for the cattle, and rain was very important. In a drought the cattle would die, and then the people would die. Because of this, the most important people among the Masai were the rain-makers, or priests who prayed for rain. The leading rain-maker was called the *Laibon*, and he acted as chief of the tribe.

According to their stories, the early Masai were led up from Lake Rudolf in the Rift Valley to the Uasin Gishu Plateau in

Kenya by a founder-chief called Maasinda. They say that Maasinda built a great ladder for the climb. From here they moved southward along the line of the Rift Valley, looking for better grazing lands. By 1600 they were living as far south as Kilimanjaro and northern Tanzania.

Most of this area was open highland country. It was good for hunting and herding cattle, but not for farming. That was why it had been left empty by the early Bantu tribes who came to East Africa before the Masai. Now the Masai were a fighting people. They were iron workers, and had great iron spears. The head of a spear was three feet long. It was sharp and heavy and could pierce any shield or even kill a buffalo. The Masai had an old story that God had given them their cattle, and that all cattle belonged to their tribe. They fought all the people round about for their herds, and would cheerfully go three hundred miles for a raid. They were invincible in the open. With their regiments of spearmen, with their long shields and their plumes waving in the sun, they terrified all who met them. But they could not conquer people who lived in wooded country and fought with bows and arrows. They remained in the open savannas, raiding from their headquarters near Lake Naivasha, proud and scornful of all other men.

Masai tribesmen

(right)
*Map of the lake region
about 1500*

(below)
*Plan of the defensive ditches
at Bigo*

N
1 mile

KATONGA RIVER

High ground   Defensive ditches

N

L. Rudolf

Some Lwo
move back
to the upper
Nile

Nilo-
Hamites
attack the
Lwo

Nilo-Hamites
(Masai)
move down
L. Rudolf and into
the Rift Valley

Mwitu
Nzige
(L. Albert)

LWO

L. Kyoga

Some Lwo
invade the Lake
Region

Some Lwo
settle on
N.E. shore
of the Nyanza

KITARO

R. Katonga

B

RWANDA
(Hutu)

R. Kagero

L. Kivu

(Tru ruled
by Chwezi)

Nyanza

(L. Victoria)

RIFT VALLEY

BURUNDI

L. Tanganyika

Movement of
Nilo-Hamites

Movement of Lwo

●B

Earthwork defences
at Bigo

0   100   200   300
Miles

The southern Nilotes: the Lwo

Some of the Nilo-Hamites, such as the Lango, the Teso and the Karamojong, instead of going south like the Masai, moved south-west towards Lake Kyoga. Here they met the Lwo-speaking Nilotes, who had moved south up the Nile from the Nilotic homeland.

The Nilo-Hamites drove out the Lwo. Some Lwo moved south to the shore of Lake Nyanza, where they live today in the Lake Province of Kenya. Others turned back to the north-west, where they are still living, in the Sudan. Still others moved into the lake region, into the part which is present-day Uganda. Here lived the early Bantu, many of whom were being ruled by the Chwezi chiefs, also known as the Hima.

These Lwo came south. They appeared to the Bantu as a strange and terrible people. Tall and dark-skinned, they were said to be as many as the grains of millet in a good harvest. Their spears were of iron—even the haft of a spear was sometimes made of iron. Nothing could stop them, and they advanced south to the Katonga River, the boundary of the Chwezi kingdom of Ruanda.

Here the Chwezi made a great effort to stop the Lwo. They built earthwork defences along the river. The biggest, with earth mounds and trenches a mile long, some dug out of the rock, was at Bigo. It guarded the most important ford on the middle Katonga. Even this did not stop the Lwo armies, however, and the Chwezi-Hutu people had to escape south into the Ruanda of today.

Bunyoro

The Lwo settled down in the north, and there founded the kingdom of Bunyoro. The Lwo chiefs of Bunyoro were of the Bito clan. Most of the Lwo soon married Bantu wives, however, and Bunyoro became a Bantu kingdom. Their kings had the title of Mukama.

The heart of Bunyoro lay south of the Kafu River, from Singo across to northern Toro. Around this country, the Nyoro set up subject kingdoms, and gave them chiefs of the Bito clan. They took many of the customs of the Chwezi, which they learned from their new subjects. Some of the new provinces were Buddu, Kyaka, Bungungu and Buruli. Later the Nyoro extended their power to Ankole in the south, to the Toro north of Ruwenzori, and to Busoga on the border of present-day Kenya. By 1600 they were the strongest empire in East Africa.

Buganda

On the north-west shore of Lake Nyanza lived a small Bantu tribe called the Ganda. They had had a legendary founder chief called Kintu, but by this time they were ruled by Bito chiefs whom they called Kabaka.

None the less, Buganda was not really part of the Nyoro Empire. In 1600 the Nyoro tried to conquer them, but they were beaten off in a great battle at Mbale. The Ganda were helped by the fishermen of the Sese Islands in the lake, and they always remembered this alliance with gratitude. The Nyoro left the Ganda and turned to fight in the south.

Then, about 1650, there began a great change. The Nyoro

crossed the Kagera River beyond Ankole, and invaded Kar-agwe. But here they were far from home, and their great army was defeated.

When the news reached Buganda, the people called for revenge on Bunyoro for past raids. Kabaka Katerega, the eleventh Ganda king, led his armies north and west, and soon doubled the size of the Ganda kingdom. After this, from 1700 to 1800, Buganda continued to grow. On the map you can see how this happened.

During this time, the Kabakas became stronger rulers. They began to live in grass-and-reed palaces in the Chwezi style. Two very harsh rulers were Kagulu and Kikulwe, but although they were hated by the people, they strengthened the kabaka-ship. Then the next step was to put an end to the system of

The growth of Buganda 1600–1800

85

allowing the provinces to be ruled by hereditary chiefs. This reform began when Kabaka Junju took the great province of Buddu from Bunyoro in about 1750. Buddu was given an appointed governor, who was no more than a civil servant. The same thing was done in other provinces. It gave the Kabaka more control in his country.

By 1800, Buganda was the strongest kingdom in the lake region. It controlled the whole western shore of Lake Nyanza from the Kagera to the Nile. Bunyoro was now only a small kingdom to the north-east.

The growth of Buganda was also helped by trade. Junju's successor, Kabaka Semakokiro, opened a long-distance trade with the Nyamwezi south of Lake Nyanza. The Nyamwezi, about whom you will read later in this chapter, already traded with the Arabs on the coast. The most important part of this trade was the export of ivory. The Ganda raided Bunyoro and beyond for ivory, and in the nineteenth century for slaves. After 1850, as you will read in Chapter 13, Arabs themselves came to Buganda. In this way, because they commanded the entrance to the lake region from the south-east, the Ganda were able to become a wealthy as well as a powerful people.

Tanzania

Away to the south-east of the lake region lies the wide land which today we call Tanzania. Most of it is a dry, wide plain with some ranges of hills in the south. Only one important river flows through it, the Rufiji. There are no marked natural features that would encourage a tribe to form a kingdom with firm frontiers, and the land was too poor for the people to farm easily. Perhaps that is why early Bantu tribes like the early Sotho and the Karanga passed straight through the country on their way south to look for better land. However, there were many herds of wild game and thousands of elephant. Tanganyika became one of the biggest sources of ivory in Africa.

After A.D. 1000 the country was inhabited by small tribes of early Bantu. Most of them had come from the Congo region. There were also a few Bushmen and early Hamites, but these were steadily driven out or absorbed by the new Iron Age peoples.

These small Bantu-speaking tribes did not have chiefs at first. They lived in small clans loosely joined together in groups. But you may remember that the early Bantu of the lake region,

Elephants in Tanzanian landscape

who had come from the Sudan, did have chiefs, even in the days before the Hima invasion. Now the Tanganyikan tribes nearest to Lake Nyanza began to adopt the idea of chiefs from the peoples of the lake region.

'Ntemi' chieftainship

This change took place because a tribe led by a chief was stronger and better organized than one without a chief. Strong groups looking for better land were able to overcome the villages to the south, and the leader would set himself up as ruler. All western Tanganyikan tribes say that their chieftainships were begun by cattle-owning strangers from the northwest. Moreover, all of them call their chiefs by the title of *Ntemi*. *Ntemi* comes from a word meaning 'to cut'—perhaps because the chief was the person who cut short discussion and came to a decision; perhaps because he was the man of the axe, a symbol of chieftainship.

In fact the Ntemi was a sort of 'divine king'. He controlled the sacred fire of the tribe, which must not go out. He controlled the forge, and the men who smelted iron for the tribe.

When he fell ill, his death was hastened, and he was buried in a special way with his servants, who were also sacrificed.

The spread of Ntemi chieftainship from north to south through western Tanganyika probably happened between about 1200 and 1500.

Unyamwezi

Most of the Ntemi kingdoms were quite small. Some had only about a thousand subjects. The largest was the kingdom of the Nyamwezi, with their allies, the Sukuma. These people lived south of Lake Nyanza and east of Burundi. They followed the custom that the son inherits from the father. They kept cattle, but these were different from the long-horned Hima cattle.

Shore of Lake Nyanza

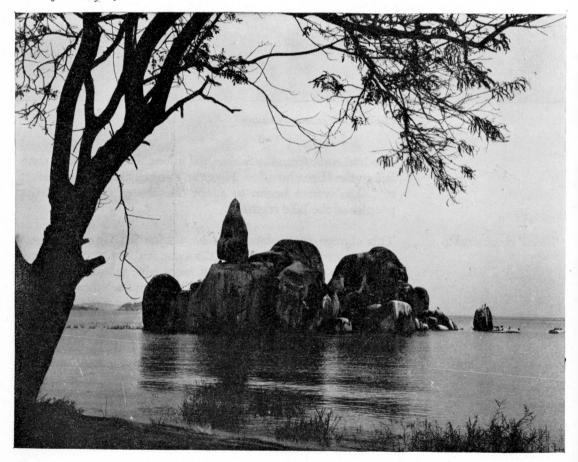

From this we know that their rulers came from the lake region before the Hima conquest.

First they extended their power southward to the Iringa highlands, where the Hehe people lived. Next, the Sukuma dominated the country east of Lake Nyanza, until then the home of pastoralists and hunters. Finally in the eighteenth century the Nyamwezi began to control Gogo country in the east.

Because of this, many tribes beyond Nyamwezi country came to be ruled by Ntemi chiefs, although they were not part of the Nyamwezi kingdom. Among these tribes were the Namwanga and the Nyakyusa in the south, the Kinga, the Bena and the Hehe in the south-east, and the Gogo in the east. Farther east still, even the Sagara and the Shambaa, only a hundred miles from the coast, began to have Ntemi chiefs by about 1750. To the north-east, of course, this influence was stopped by the presence of the warrior Nilo-Hamites such as the Masai.

Ivory trade

In time the Nyamwezi became a great trading people. By 1750 they had learned that the Swahili and Arabs of the coast would pay well in cloth for ivory.

The ivory trade needed organized rule: elephants had to be hunted, and all the tusks brought in; carriers had to be recruited and sent in large parties to the coast; and armed guards had to go with the trading parties to protect them. The Nyamwezi, being the largest kingdom not too far from the coastal markets, became the ivory traders of East Africa. After 1800, large parties with hundreds of men made the long, hot march from Unyamwezi to the sea.

Nyamwezi men became known as the finest carriers in East Africa. Nyamwezi children used to start practising with small tusks on their heads from an early age.

Kenya

We now come to the remaining part of East Africa. This is present-day Kenya, between the highlands and the sea. Most of the present Bantu inhabitants arrived about 1600 from Tanganyika to the south. They settled in the well-wooded country around Mount Kenya. The most important tribes were the Kikuyu and the Kamba inland, and the Taita and the Nyika near the sea.

These tribes remained without chiefs until recent times.

They were too far north for the Ntemi system to reach them. Their country was isolated from the rest of Bantu Africa. To the north was the dry country where the nomadic Somali and Galla lived. To the west were the warrior Masai in the highlands above the Rift Valley, and to the east was the sea. South, from where they had come, was Mount Kilimanjaro, and beyond it the dry coastal plain.

The Kikuyu

When the Kikuyu first arrived in this country, they found already living there an early Bantu tribe called Ndorobo. These Ndorobo were a primitive people who used stone as well as iron. They made pit-dwellings covered with roofs of wild banana leaves, and lived by hunting in the forest. They buried their dead carefully, and worshipped the ancestral spirits.

The Kikuyu, who were cattle farmers at first, lived in more open country, and were friendly towards the Ndorobo. In alliance with them, and even with the Masai, they fought a Galla invasion from the north and drove them out. The Kikuyu

Early photograph of an elephant hunt

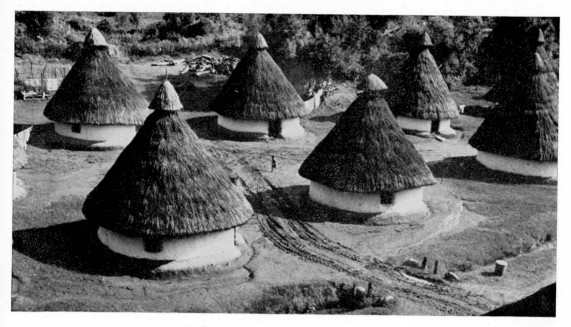

A Kikuyu village

have a story that before the war their leaders asked the advice of Supi, a famous medicine-man. Supi told the Ndorobo to bring sandals made of leather with hair on both sides; the Masai had to bring a bull whose dung was white; while the Kikuyu were instructed to find a rare mole called a *huko*. The Ndorobo made their sandals from the ears of a donkey; the Masai brought a bull fed only on milk; and the Kikuyu found their mole. They then went into battle, each tribe with its special charm, and won the war.

However, the Masai now turned on the Kikuyu and began to capture their herds. The Kikuyu retreated to the forests, and began to clear them in order to cultivate grain crops. The Ndorobo, who lived in the forest, were now driven out to the north, and their numbers decreased. The Masai repeatedly attacked the Kikuyu, but the Kikuyu, armed with bows and arrows, fought them from the forest and drove them back. By 1800 they were the strongest tribe around Mount Kenya, and worshipped a god called Ngai who, they said, lived in the mountain.

Mount Kenya

The Kamba

South-east of Mount Kenya lived the Kamba. Like the Nyamwezi inland, they were a trading people. To the Arabs on the coast they sold ivory and cattle. From them they bought cotton, glass beads, copper wire and salt. They sold these goods from the coast to the Kikuyu for food. Kamba country was dry, and famine frequent.

Engaruka

Before leaving this chapter on the peoples of East Africa, you should read about one mystery that has puzzled historians. This mystery is the remains of a town at Engaruka, twenty miles south of Lake Natron in the Rift Valley. Terraces cover the hill-slopes, and on them are the remains of over six thousand rough stone houses. The town was destroyed about three hundred years ago, probably by the Masai, and its inhabitants driven out. Who were they? Of what race and language? Perhaps one day we shall know. Today we believe that Engaruka was built by the early Hamites who lived in East Africa before the Bantu came (see Chapter 10, Book One).

An account of *Ntemi* chieftainship

Turi set out with the men of Vuga, a very great army, young men and elders, with two war-horns and his flute and his signal-horn. . . .

And they came to that place with song and dance, and every man vaunted his prowess and glorified his country and boasted of his pre-eminence and rank.

And Turi, their headman, was received with shouts of applause. And he proclaimed his skill in his craft, and glorified the fire of his forge, and boasted how he slew the men of Pare with his spear, and how he beat out arrows and axes and hammers and knives. . . . And he boasted that he was rich in oxen and goats and sheep, and he claimed that it was he who protected all the people and cared for them with gentle kindness. And at every word he asked his people, 'Is this that I say true or false?' and his people responded with one voice, 'It is true.'

.   .   .   .

Whoever comes to this country of Usambara must admit that he is Turi's man. That clan holds the country because God gave them the gift of working iron, and skill in war. . . . None but they have ornaments, none dares to boast himself a son of the country.

from the *Habari za Wakilindi*

East African Time Chart

Date	The Lake Region	Kenya and Tanzania	East Coast
A.D.	Possibly some early Hamitic Stone Age inhabitants.	Interior inhabited by small groups of brown-skinned early Hamites of Stone Age culture.	Some Indian traders visit east coast. *Periplus of Erythrean Sea* written by Greek trader.
100			
200			
300			
400			Rhapta and other 'Azanian' coastal towns flourishing on Arabian and Indian trade.
500			
600			The *Hijra* of Mohammed.
700	Some early Bantu settlers had probably arrived by this time.	Early Iron Age Bantu begin to arrive from the Congo region.	Arab and Persian settlements begin as far south as Kilwa.
800			Decline of Rhapta and other African coast towns.
900			
1000			El Masoudi makes first report of black people living on the east coast. Kilwa grows into a large town.
1100			Kilwa gains control of Sofala.
1200			'Golden Age' of Kilwa begins.
1300		Spread of *Ntemi* chieftainship from Karagwe begins. Galla migration through Somaliland and northern Kenya begins.	
1400			Kilwa begins to decline.
1500	Galla meet Sidama north of Lake Rudolf. Results: 1. Chwezi conquest of lake region. 2. Nilo-Hamites formed. 3. Lwo invasion of lake region.	Early Hamitic town of Engaruka flourishing. Nilo-Hamites (e.g. Masai) move south, destroying Engaruka.	Rise of Pate. Sofala becomes independent. Portuguese arrive on east coast. Kilwa and other towns captured.
1600	Kingdom of Bunyoro established. Nyoro defeated in Karagwe. Kabaka Katerega leads Ganda.	Chiefless tribes (e.g. Kikuyu) move into N.E. Kenya. Wars with Galla and Masai.	Fort Jesus built at Mombasa. Seif bin Sultan attacks Mombasa, takes Fort Jesus. Portuguese driven from east coast north of Mozambique.
1700	Growth of Buganda. Buganda the strongest kingdom in the lake region. Trade with Arabs develops.	Nyamwezi begin trading between lake region and the coast. Ngoni groups conquer tribes in S. Tanzania. Arab traders move inland.	Sayyid Said, Sultan of Oman, comes to Zanzibar. Rapid growth of slave trade.
1800			
1900			

11 Bantu from the Congo highlands

Let us now look back and consider the movement of the Bantu peoples as a whole.

The homeland, or what is sometimes called the cradleland, of the Bantu-speaking peoples had been the western Sudan, towards what is today the Cameroons. After learning about the manufacture and use of iron, the Bantu-speaking peoples moved south. They moved, you may remember, along two main routes.

First were the cattle-owning tribes. These tribes mostly had chiefs, and generally followed the custom of the son inheriting from the father. They had first travelled east across the Sudan, and then south, entering the lake region. Some early tribes, such as the Karanga, Sotho, Abenguni and Venda, went even farther south, past the lakes, beyond the Zambezi and even to South Africa. Other later tribes such as the Iru, the Hutu and the Ganda settled down in the lake region.

Next we noticed the early Bantu of Tanganyika. These tribes followed the custom of the son inheriting from the father, but they did not keep cattle, and at first they did not have chiefs. These early tribes came, not from the lake region to the north, but from the Congo in the west.

Other tribes from the Congo

We shall now read about other tribes which came to south-east Africa from the Congo in the west. These Bantu-speaking people had also come from the western Sudan long ago, but their route of migration had been along the Upper Congo basin. In the west and centre of the Congo basin there is dense forest, but these tribes kept to the eastern highlands as much as possible. At last they passed south of Lake Tanganyika and moved east across the Lualaba. They came in the end to north-eastern Zambia and Lake Malawi.

Most of these tribes did not keep cattle. They followed the custom that the son inherits from the mother, and goes to live at his wife's village. Generally they had chiefs.

Malawi

The Malawi are those tribes which settled along the east and south of Lake Malawi, and in between the Luangwa and Zambezi Rivers, before the Abenguni came. At first they were one

Fishing canoes on the shore of Lake Malawi

tribe, divided into clans. The chiefs of the three largest clans were called Karonga, Undi and Mwase. Their old stories say that at one time they lived near the Luba tribe of the Upper Congo. They reached the north of Lake Malawi some time after 1400.

Some of the Malawi settled down at the north end of Lake Malawi under Karonga. They liked the fertile valleys where crops grew well. There was plenty of rain because wind from the far-off ocean blew over the mountains. Iron was to be found in the district. Later they learned fishing from the earliest Bantu inhabitants, such as the Nkonde, the Henga and the Tumbuka.

Most of the Malawi moved farther south to the country west of the Shire River. By this time they had lived long enough near Lake Malawi to call themselves the 'Lake People', which in their language is *Mang'anja*. Their chiefs were called Mkanda. They lived peacefully in their neat villages, cultivating their fields of millet and banana, looking after their flocks of sheep and goats, and making their excellent iron-work.

Cewa kingdoms

About 1500 the Mang'anja were increasing in numbers, and some clans moved away to the west. These clans called themselves Cewa, although they were still of the Malawi tribe and spoke nearly the same language.

First, there were the Cewa led by Mwase. They went up to the uninhabited Luangwa valley. They made the chief's village at Kasungu, and still live in that district today. Other Malawi calling themselves Cewa moved farther west and settled down at

Petauke. They also hunted and farmed and lived peacefully.

Beyond the Luangwa lived some early Bantu who had come from Katanga country a long time before. The Cewa mixed peacefully with these people, and formed a new tribe living beside their own, called the Nsenga. The Nsenga chiefs were named Kalindawalu.

There were many elephants in Malawi country. Because of this, the Arabs and Portuguese came to trade there later on. When they came for ivory they also took away people captive. That is why the Malawi suffered badly from the slave trade, but this did not happen until after 1800.

Bemba

After the Malawi, another people came from the southern Congo to the north-east Zambian plateau. These were the Bemba. The Bemba did not go as far as Lake Malawi, but stayed west of the Luangwa River.

The Bemba homeland, which they call *Kola*, was in northern Angola. The Kasai River runs from there into the Congo, but the Bemba stayed on the plateau. They were not a river people. They spoke a Luba language, and did not keep cattle. They followed the custom of the son inheriting from the mother.

The Bemba had chiefs from early times. These chiefs were strong and sometimes harsh rulers. The founder chief, who was called Nshinga, may have lived about 1500. A later chief called Kapopo was an unpopular ruler, and some of the tribe fled away to settle on the Lualaba. Here developed the Bemba tribe as we know it.

The Bemba conquered the valley people and learned to speak their language, which is Cibemba today. From this time, their chiefs took the title *Mukulu* or *Mukulumpe*, which means 'The Great One'.

About 1670, their chief was Mulopwe. He tried to make the people work hard, cutting grass in the dry season. The people became discontented, and his sons protested. Mulopwe threatened to kill one of his sons called Chiti. So Chiti with his brother Nkole led their clans away, south of Lake Mweru. Here they defeated the Shila in battle, and crossed the Luapula.

Chitimukulu

After the Bemba had crossed the Luapula, small clans broke away to find lands of their own. There was plenty of land, for the only people living in this region were Bushmen. Among the

Bemba clans which now made separate tribes were the Ushi, the Chishinga, the Bisa and the Senga. The Bisa went south of Lake Bangweulu. The Senga moved east, up to the Muchinga escarpment.

For a short time the main Bemba tribe went south-east into the Muchingas and tried to cross the Luangwa. Here they found the Nsenga and the Cewa under Mwase, who had arrived a hundred years before. The Bemba fought the Cewa and won this small war, but Chiti was killed.

Now Chiti's nephew, according to Bemba custom, became paramount chief, and took the title of Chitimukulu. He led the tribe north across the Chambeshi River, and finally settled on the plateau to the north. Here the Bemba became a powerful nation. They ruled the country between Lakes Bangweulu, Mweru and Tanganyika and the headwaters of the Luangwa River.

The Malawi, Luba and Luyi migrations

The Lunda dispersal

Meanwhile, another great Bantu-speaking tribe had been growing powerful in the southern Congo. This was the Luba nation,
about whom we read in Chapter 7. The Luba, like their cousins,
the Bemba, had come south from the Cameroons to the Angola
highlands where the Kasai begins. They had left the Cameroons
later than other Bantu, and were possibly related to the great
Yoruba nation, a Negro tribe in Nigeria (Chapter 6). Later
the Luba moved away from Angola. By 1600 the Luba kingdom
extended from the Lubilashi to the Lualaba River.

Before long an important new branch of the Luba was
formed to the south. This was the Lunda, who have a story
that Iala Mwaku was chief of a Luba clan called Bungu.
About 1600, when Iala Mwaku was an old man, he was badly
treated by his three sons. Iala therefore said that, when he died,
the chieftainship must pass to his grand-daughter, a young
princess named Lueji. For this purpose, he gave Lueji the *lukano*
bracelet, the symbol of royal power.

Iala's sons were so angry that they took their clans away from
Buluba. One of them, Chinguri, went as far as Luanda and met
the Portuguese there in 1609. Another, Chinyama, went south-
west and founded the Lovale tribe.

Meanwhile, Lueji had become queen, and married a Luba
hunter named Chibinda Ilunga. She presented Chibinda with
the *lukano* bracelet which gave him the chief's authority. At
about this time the people of Lueji and Chibinda began to call
themselves the Lunda tribe.

Chibinda's grandson, Iavo Naweji, extended the Lunda kingdom to the south. This high sandy plateau, the Congo-Zambezi
watershed, was then empty of people. The Lunda clans which
now settled there were led by Musokantanda, Kanongesha and
Ishinde. The Lunda people were now a powerful empire with
vast lands, and Iavo Naweji was given the title of 'lord of
wealth', or *mwata yamvo*.

Although the country was not very good for farming, there
were quantities of ivory. The Lunda also discovered new supplies of copper ore, which they called *katanga*. They became
good copper workers. They made copper bracelets and ankle
rings, and copper bars cross-shaped in section. Copper and ivory
were sent to the west coast Portuguese, in exchange for cloth
and beads.

X-shaped copper bar

The Luapula Lunda

Some time after Iavo Naweji died, the Lunda attacked the Shila in the Luapula valley, and conquered them. This was about 1740. Bilonda, a grandson of Iavo, was made ruler of the Luapula settlement, and took the title of Kazembe.

Bilonda even went with an army across the north-eastern plateau as far as the Luangwa. But the Bemba clans were already settling there, and in any case the Lunda preferred the Luapula valley with its rich soil and its fish supplies.

Mwata Yamvo traded with Luanda. Kazembe did the same, but he also tried to open trade with the east coast. He had heard of the Arabs and the Portuguese there. In 1798 a Portuguese traveller, Dr Lacerda, came to his village from Tete, but he died of fever. The Bemba and Bisa were unfriendly to travellers. After 1850, however, Arab traders from Kilwa and Zanzibar came to live on the Luapula, and an ivory, copper and slave trade began.

The Luyi

West of Luba country, yet another tribe, the Luyi, was moving south. *Baluyi* means 'river people', and the Luyi had for some time been living in the Kasai River valley.

The Luyi were separate from the Luba, but were related to them. An old story says that the two tribes had the same founder chief, who was a woman called Mbuywamwamba. The Luyi, like the Luba, did not keep cattle. Unlike them, they did not even have chiefs to begin with.

Coming south from the Kasai some time after 1500, the Luyi settled in the valley plain of the Upper Zambezi. Here they started to have chiefs, of whom the first was called Mboo. They also learned from the Ila on the Kafue plateau the practice of keeping cattle. With fish, cattle and the fertile land of the floodplain, the Luyi became a wealthy and powerful nation. They subdued several of the surrounding tribes, and even fought the Lovale in the north.

Their greatest ruler was Mulambwa, the twelfth chief, who ruled from 1812 to 1830. Mulambwa made good laws for the governing of the country, and refused to talk with the Mambari slave traders who came from the Angola coast.

After Mulambwa died the Luyi kingdom was divided, and it was easily conquered by the fighting Kololo who came up from the south in 1838. In the next chapter we shall read about these and other warlike peoples from the south.

12 Warrior kingdoms of the south

Let us go back for a moment, and remember that some early Bantu-speaking groups had passed through the Rift Valley, crossed the Zambezi, moved along the edge of the Kalahari, and settled in South Africa.

Some of these groups became the Sotho-speaking tribes, who lived on the tableland between the Drakensberg Mountains and south-west Africa. Others became the Nguni-speaking tribes, or Abenguni, who lived on the southern slopes of the Drakensberg, and in the coastal lowlands. The Sotho and the Abenguni reached the southern part of South Africa between 1600 and 1700.

After 1700, the Abenguni were advancing through Natal. About 1780 they met the Dutch settlers who were moving eastwards from the Cape. A number of wars were fought with these Dutch farmers, who were called Boers, and the Abenguni advance was stopped.

The Dutch come to South Africa

Dutch settlers had come to the Cape of Good Hope in 1652. Like the Portuguese, they wanted a place for their ships to find fresh water and fruit on the way to the spice islands of the east. The Portuguese then controlled the east coast of Africa, so the Dutch chose the Cape.

An old Boer farmhouse

The climate was so good for white people, that before long the Dutch were establishing farms east of the Cape. They found it was easy to drive out the Stone Age Bushmen and even the Hottentots who had been living there before they came.

About 1780 the Dutch Boers met the first of the Abenguni people, members of the Xhosa tribe, along the Great Fish River. The Xhosa and the Boers fought wars, because they each wanted grazing land for their cattle.

The Abenguni people were now in trouble. Their numbers were increasing, but they could not find new land. The Boers stopped them in the west, and the Sotho blocked them in the north. The Abenguni now began to fight among themselves.

Shaka and the *mfecane* wars

One of the strongest of the Abenguni tribes was the Mtetwa. Chief of the Mtetwa was Dingiswayo, a great warrior. Dingiswayo trained his soldiers strictly, fed them on beef to make them strong, and armed them with a short broad-bladed spear for stabbing and a thick ox-hide shield. He taught them to fight in a special formation, shaped like the horns of a bull.

The army was divided into regiments according to clans. The leader of one of these regiments was Shaka, of the Zulu clan. *Zulu* means 'people of the sky'.

When Dingiswayo died in 1818, Shaka, with the help of his Zulus, made himself the chief of the Mtetwa. Now the Mtetwa came to be called Zulu. Shaka led the Zulus on conquering raids: north to Swaziland, west into the Drakensberg and south against the Xhosa. The Zulus were undefeated. The terrible Shaka had hundreds of thousands of cattle in his kraals.

The wars which Shaka began spread beyond the Drakensberg as far as the Vaal River. The tribes called these wars the *mfecane*, or the 'crushing'. They were not the work of the Zulus alone, however. Other Abenguni and Sotho groups, driven out by Shaka, set out to travel far away, fighting and destroying as they went.

Let us look at the brief histories of these tribes.

Late 17th century Dutch painting of the Cape of Good Hope, showing Table Mountain

The Kololo conquest of Barotseland

Some of the Abenguni, led by a Zulu general called Mzilikazi, crossed the mountains and fought the Sotho. Many of the Sotho fled westward. Among them was a band of warriors led by a woman named Mantati. This band or horde, for they were many, prepared to attack the Tswana near Kuruman, but they were routed in a great battle by the Griqua. A small group called Kololo, whose leader was Sebitwane, escaped to the north.

The Kololo spent fifteen years from 1823 to 1838 moving north through the fringes of the Kalahari to the Zambezi. They crossed the Zambezi, defeated the Toka, and moved up to the Barotse plain.

Here the Luyi had quarrelled among themselves since the

death of Mulambwa, so they were easily conquered by the Kololo in four battles. Some of the Luyi, however, escaped north of the Kabompo River. Among them was a boy who was later to become the great chief Lewanika.

The Kololo, under Sebitwane and his son, Sekeletu, ruled Barotseland well until 1865. Then the Luyi, or the Lozi, as they were now called, rebelled and overthrew the Kololo. During that time the people of Barotseland had come to speak the Sotho language and to have many Sotho customs.

The Ngoni migration

An important Abenguni group, which broke away from Natal about the same time as the Kololo, were the Ngoni. They were led by Zwangendaba. This great soldier and chief, still a young man, had refused to submit to Shaka's tyranny. He and his ally, Zwide of the Ndwandwe, fought the Zulus but were defeated. Zwide was captured and put to death, but Zwangendaba and about a thousand of his followers escaped.

Although they were few in number, the Ngoni conquered all the people they met on their northward march, and soon had gathered a large and disciplined army.

About 1830 they came to the Rozwi kingdom in Mashonaland. The Ngoni spread fire and slaughter through Mashonaland, burning villages and killing the Rozwi king. They did not stop to settle in the country they had pillaged; instead they crossed the Zambezi near Zumbo in 1835, and marched north. This march took them through Malawi country, up the shore of Lake Malawi. Beyond Lake Malawi, in Ufipa, Zwangendaba died.

Now the Ngoni could not agree who should inherit the chieftainship. The tribe split up, different parts following different leaders.

Mpezeni turned south-west. At once he met the Bemba, and was defeated by them. It was the first great battle that the Ngoni had lost; but you must remember that the tribe had just broken up, and was not as strong as before. So Mpezeni moved south and conquered the Nsenga, before settling in Cewa country south of the Luangwa.

Zulu chief in full war dress

A Zulu kraal

Mbelwa turned south-east and settled in the hills above Lake Malawi, driving out the Tonga, the Henga and the Malawi tribes.

Gomani took his followers round the north of Lake Malawi and settled north of the Rovuma River, in present-day Tanzania.

Ngoni language and custom

You may remember that the Ngoni, when they left Natal under Zwangendaba, had numbered only about one thousand men. Now they had become a great nation or group of tribes conquering and settling in large parts of north-eastern Zambia, Malawi and Tanzania.

This had happened because, when the Ngoni defeated another tribe, they took the younger men captive and trained them to be Ngoni warriors. They also married wives from the subject tribes. These wives became the mothers of Ngoni children. The children learnt the language of their mothers, so that the Ngoni language slowly disappeared. The different Ngoni groups speak the language of the people they conquered— Cewa, Tumbuka, Nsenga, Mang'anga (or Nyanja) and Yao.

Much of Ngoni custom, on the other hand, has lived on. They keep cattle, and the son inherits from the father. They still build their villages in the old Ngoni way. Most important, the Ngoni system of chieftainship has continued.

Strong chieftainship

When the Ngoni came to southern Tanganyika, they had met those tribes about some of whom we read in Chapter 10—the Nyakyusa, Namwanga, Kimba and Sanga. These people had become used to *Ntemi* chieftainship, which they had learned from the Nyamwezi-Sukuma peoples in the past (see p. 87).

In spite of this, the southern Tanganyika tribes were still small and poorly organized. As a result of the Ngoni conquest, some of these tribes were forced into stronger and larger groups under powerful Ngoni chiefs.

Outside the area of Ngoni conquest, other tribes united in order to resist them. The first of these groupings was that of the Sangu under Chief Merere. His capital was at Utengele in the southern Tanganyika highlands. Next were the Hehe who, under Muyungumba, became strong enough to check Chipeta's Ngoni in the east. In the north, the Nyamwezi continued to be one of the strongest tribes in Tanganyika.

This strengthening of Tanganyika tribes had important

The migrations of the southern Bantu

effects when Arab traders came to the region soon afterwards. Some tribes were strong enough to resist the Arabs; others began to make war on weaker tribes, and sell their captives to slave caravans. We shall read about these events in the next chapter.

First of all, however, we must look briefly at one more important tribe which went north from Natal as the result of Shaka's *mfecane* wars.

The Ndebele

Lobengula and his wife

The leader of one of Shaka's armies was Mzilikazi, a great Zulu general. His task was to make war on the Sotho, and terrible battles were fought in the valleys of the Drakensberg.

Now it was Shaka's rule that all cattle taken in war should become his own property. There were huge herds in the royal kraals. After one of his raids, Mzilikazi kept the cattle for his own followers without telling Shaka. The king was enraged and ordered the death of all concerned. Mzilikazi decided not to fight Shaka, but escaped with his army beyond the Drakensberg to the north.

This fighting group came to be known as Ndebele, or Matabele. They made war on the people south and north of the Vaal River, and left charred and smoking villages for hundreds of miles around.

The Boers came north to the Vaal River in 1836. The Ndebele attacked them in two battles, but were defeated by the Boer guns. Mzilikazi then went farther north, to be out of reach of the advancing white men. He crossed the Limpopo and made his capital at Inyati near the Matopo Hills.

From here the Ndebele raided the Shona peoples. They killed them or enslaved them, and took their cattle away. The Rozwi kingdom had been destroyed by the Ngoni ten years before. Now the Shona were finally terrorized and broken up.

The Ndebele also raided the Tswana to the south-west and the Lozi and the Toka across the Zambezi. However, the Ndebele did not try to rule these people or to build an empire. They liked war and plenty of cattle in their kraals.

After Mzilikazi died in 1868, Lobengula became king. There was no change in the Ndebele way of life, and the raids went on as before.

South-Central African Time Chart

Date	Southern Africa	Mashonaland	East Coast
A.D.	Sparsely inhabited by Stone Age Bushmen and Hottentots.	Inhabited by Bushmen, with some early Hamites, all of Stone Age culture.	Some Indian traders had long been visiting the east coast.
100			*Periplus of Erythrean Sea* written by Greek trader.
200			
300			Rhapta and other 'Azanian' coastal towns flourishing on Arabian and Indian trade.
400			
500			
600		Early Iron Age Bantu settlers probably arriving.	Arab and Persian settlements begin as far south as Kilwa.
700			Decline of Rhapta and other African coast towns.
800		Early Karanga (Shona) moving south from Lake Tanganyika.	
900	First southern Bantu move south of the Limpopo at about this time.		El Masoudi makes first report of black people living on the east coast.
1000		Karanga cross the Zambezi. Karanga kingdom set up between Zambezi and Limpopo. 'Acropolis' building begun at Great Zimbabwe. Arabs visit Mashonaland. Trade begins with Sofala.	Kilwa grows into a large town.
1100	Early Sotho and Nguni groups cross the Limpopo southward.		Kilwa gains control of Sofala.
1200			'Golden Age' of Kilwa begins.
1300	Sotho and Abenguni slowly move southward, driving out Bushmen.		
1400		Mutota becomes first Monomotapa.	Kilwa begins to decline. Rise of Pate. Sofala becomes independent.
1500		Rozwi split away under Changa. Great temple begun at Zimbabwe. Acropolis completed. Portuguese come to Mashonaland. Silveira martyred.	Portuguese arrive on east coast. Kilwa and other towns captured. Fort Jesus built at Mombasa.
1600	Sotho established in Botswana and along the Orange River.	Zimba raids. Arab influence returns. Monomatapa drives out Portuguese. Rozwi empire established. Great temple completed.	Zimba raiders destroyed. Seif bin Sultan attacks Mombasa, takes Fort Jesus. Portuguese driven from east coast north of Mozambique.
1700	Abenguni in Natal, now meeting Dutch settlers from the Cape.		
1800	Rise of Shaka. *Mfecane* wars. Ngoni, Kololo, Ndebele move north.	Ngoni invasion. Rozwi kingdom destroyed.	Sayyid Said, Sultan of Oman, comes to Zanzibar. Rapid growth of slave trade.
1900			

13 New trade begins in East Africa

For a very long time, traders had come to the east coast of Africa. You may remember that by 600 B.C., and perhaps earlier, traders from the east had been using the monsoon wind for sailing.

Then Arabs and Persians had settled on the coast before A.D. 1000. They built towns which grew into fine cities. After them came the Portuguese in 1498, and from 1500 to 1700 the Portuguese ruled the Arab coastal towns.

The fortress of San Sebastian, Mozambique

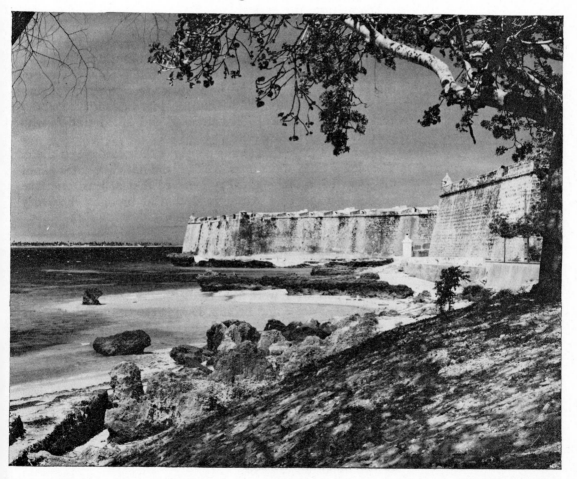

We have seen that after 1700 most of the Arab towns were independent again, though the Portuguese still kept Mozambique and the lower Zambezi valley. For over a hundred years the towns went on with their trade as before. Often they fought with one another. Mostly they were under the control of the Sultan of Oman.

Through all this time the trade took place only along the coast. Africans from inland brought their ivory down to the sea. Large expeditions sometimes came from the Nyamwezi kingdom to buy iron and cotton and glass beads from the Swahili and Arabs, and then travel back inland.

People from the coast did not usually go into the interior. In Mashonaland, it is true, Arabs and Portuguese went to live and trade until the Rozwi drove them out in 1693. They were there for the gold. North of the Zambezi this did not happen, because there was little gold, distances were great and parts of the country were dry and forbidding. In northern Tanganyika and Kenya, the Nilo-Hamites, who had arrived about 1600, were unfriendly. They attacked and killed traders who passed through their country.

Because of these things, the people of the coast stayed there. They knew little of the interior. They did not even know about the great lakes, although they believed that at least one lake existed, because the Bantu traders who brought the ivory sometimes talked of the inland waters.

One reason for the decline of the Portuguese had been that other countries were sending ships to the Far East, and taking away the trade of the Portuguese.

These countries were the Netherlands, where the Dutch people live, France and Britain. During the two hundred years between 1600 and 1800, they built up great empires overseas. Britain and France especially became powerful in North America and the Far East.

These countries did not try to make empires in Africa, though they had trading posts on the west coast. This was because they did not think Africa had great wealth. Moreover travel inside Africa was difficult and dangerous, and it was easier to go to other places first.

After about 1750, however, the situation began to change, for two important reasons.

First, because of their empires and growing trade, these countries began to grow richer. In Britain and France especially, machines were invented and factories were built. These could produce many more goods than the old way of working by hand.

People in these countries now wanted to buy more goods from abroad, like cotton to make into cloth, and palm oil for their machines. Such goods are called raw materials. They also wanted more food from abroad, like sugar and spices, to feed the increasing numbers of their population.

Besides buying from abroad, the new industrial countries wanted to be able to sell the things they had made. Their factories produced more goods than people wanted at home, so they needed to find people who would buy them abroad. After a time, traders in these countries came to see that there were many people in Africa who would buy their cloth and iron and other goods.

Sugar plantations

The second change was the growing demand for sugar in Europe. Sugar-cane grows in a hot, damp climate. This climate is found in the West Indies. When the people in Britain and France grew wealthier and more in number, traders found that they needed to buy more sugar from the West Indies. They made bigger sugar plantations, and grew more and more sugar-cane.

The people of the West Indies were not numerous enough to do the work. But Europeans do not like manual labour in a hot climate. Traders therefore went to Africa, where people are used to a hot climate. They went to the chiefs and took people away as slaves, paying for them with cloth and other goods. Then they brought these people in ships to the sugar islands, and made them work on the plantations. In this way, as we have read in Chapter 8, the slave trade to the West Indies developed.

After about 1770, people in Europe began to see that slave trading was wrong. Britain stopped trading in slaves after 1807, when a law was passed making such trading illegal. During the next fifty years, the British Government persuaded other European countries to stop it as well. Soon the slave trade on the west coast was ended.

Unfortunately the slave trade in East Africa went on, because the Africans were unable or unwilling to keep the Arabs out, and because Britain could not persuade the Arabs to give it up.

Arab slave trade

For a very long time, a few Africans each year had been taken away as slaves from the east coast towns. There were no sugar plantations in Arabia or Persia, but it had always been the custom for rich men to have slaves to be servants in the house and garden.

The number of slaves taken from the east coast in this way had always been small, and they were captured from villages near the coast, not from inland. That is one reason why the Bantu had so little to do with the Swahili. They were afraid of being taken captive, so they kept away from the coast.

Then there were two important developments which made the Arabs want to trade inland. The first of these was the policy of Sayyid Said at Zanzibar. The second was the growing demand for ivory.

Bateele, or Muscat Arab vessel, used in the slave trade

An old elaborate Arab tomb in Zanzibar

Sayyid Said

Since the Portuguese left, there had been quarrels between East African towns. Zanzibar had grown more wealthy and important. Mombasa with its great fort was always a strong town. The Sultan of Oman found it difficult to control the East African coast.

In 1804, Sayyid Said became Sultan of Oman. He was a strong, ambitious man. He wanted to be master of the whole Indian Ocean trade. Zanzibar was loyal to him, but he soon found that Mombasa was not. With its proud rulers of the Mazrui family, Mombasa was determined to be independent. In 1823 the Mazrui even tried to win British support, but they gave up when they found that the British were against the slave trade.

After many attempts, Sayyid Said at last forced Mombasa to submit in 1837. Three years later he left his home in Oman, and came to live in Zanzibar. He knew that he had to do this if he was to control the east coast towns and Indian Ocean trade.

Clove plantations

Now Sayyid Said resolved to make Zanzibar as rich as possible through trade. There was the ivory trade already, but ivory came from inland, and not from Zanzibar itself. Sayyid Said thought that cloves would grow well in Zanzibar.

Clove plantation and cloves

Ivory

Cloves are a sweet-smelling spice much liked by people in Europe. The Sultan started some clove plantations after 1840, and encouraged others to do the same in Zanzibar and Pemba Island. In a few years there were many clove plantations.

Now cloves have to be harvested twice a year, and much labour is needed to cultivate them. As a result the Arab planters soon began to send expeditions into the interior of East Africa to buy slaves.

Before long the number of slaves being collected in East African towns was greatly increased. Most of them were brought to the markets at Kilwa, Zanzibar and Pemba Island. The slaves who could not be sold for plantation work were put on ships and taken to Arabia and Persia.

The second reason why the Arabs on the coast wanted to trade more inland was that people in other countries needed more ivory.

The population in Europe was increasing, and many people

were growing richer. They were able to buy more goods made of ivory. Ivory was used in making parts of musical instruments, especially piano keys. It was also used for brush handles and billiard balls and furniture decoration. Ivory therefore became more valuable. Sayyid Said and other Arabs started to bring more and more ivory from the interior. As the trade of Zanzibar increased, some Arabs became very rich. More Indians, whom the Swahili called 'Banyans', came to settle in Zanzibar. They acted as bankers and lent money to Arabs who wanted to start plantations or send out trading expeditions.

These expeditions went farther and farther into the interior, sometimes for hundreds of miles.

Trade routes

The earliest trade routes used by the Arabs were from Pangani and Bagamoyo opposite Zanzibar and Pemba Island.

The route from Pangani went two hundred miles north-west to Chaga and south Masai country, near Kilimanjaro. Here there was much game and there were great herds of elephant.

In 1850 an expedition of a thousand men set out from Pangani. There were the Arab leaders riding on donkeys. There were many bearers, Swahili and Bantu, carrying food for the journey and goods to trade with. These goods were mostly cloth and ironware and glass beads, and were worth about £4,000. Then came armed soldiers, carrying guns and spears, to protect the travellers from attack. Some tribes, like the Masai, did not like traders, and tried to stop them passing through their country.

After some months inland, the expedition came back to Pangani with many elephant tusks, some rhinoceros horn, and some bags of hippopotamus teeth.

Sometimes it was possible to send two expeditions in the same year. An average of 35,000 lb. of ivory passed through Pangani every year.

The second early trade route used by Arabs went west from Bagamoyo. This route was long and difficult. It passed through dry country where travellers became hot and thirsty. Then, after reaching the Upper Rufiji River, it went through Ugogo to Unyanyembe, about five hundred miles from the coast.

Unyanyembe, which was near modern Tabora, was in the heart of Nyamwezi country. The Nyamwezi were a strong tribe, and were able to bring slaves as well as ivory to the Arab

traders. It became a big trading centre. The journey from the
coast took many weeks, and it was not easy to return the same
season. The Arabs made a settlement at Unyanyembe. Some
Arabs made their homes there, and did not return to the coast.

Farther inland

In their search for ivory, the Arabs went even beyond Unyanyembe.

First, they travelled northward, round the south and west
shores of Lake Nyanza. This was the lake region. Here the
Ganda people had broken up the Nyoro Empire and became
the strongest kingdom. Arab traders first came to the Ganda
capital in 1843.

Next, the Arabs travelled from Unyanyembe to Lake Tanganyika. On the shore of the lake, in south Burundi, they made
a settlement at Ujiji. After 1851, they crossed the lake on boats
and went into Congo country, capturing slaves. They even
reached the Lualaba, which is the Upper Congo River.

Third, the Arabs found their way round the south of Lake
Tanganyika, to Lunda country on the Luapula. They made a
settlement at Kazembe's village. Here there was a great deal
of ivory, and also copper from the Katanga west of the Luapula.

These were the main Arab trade routes. They were mostly covered by expeditions from Zanzibar.

Other routes

There was one other important trade route. This went from Kilwa, south-west across the Rovuma River, to the south end of Lake Malawi. Arabs crossed the lake in boats to Kota Kota. From there, some went across north-eastern Zambia to Kazembe's. In Nyasa country, again, the trade was mainly for ivory and slaves. After 1860, the Yao became a slave-raiding tribe, and sold their captives to the Arabs. The Portuguese also sent some slaves down to Mozambique.

Another Arab trade route went from Bagamoyo to the north end of Lake Malawi. There Arabs made a settlement, in Ngonde country. Some travelled from there, north of Lubemba, to the Luapula.

You can see these routes on the map on p. 118. They were mostly made by Arab traders between 1840 and 1860.

A carved doorway in Zanzibar

Map labels:
- R. Nile
- L. Rudolf
- Mwitu Nzige
- BUNYORO
- Mt Elgon △
- Mt Kenya △
- Stanley Falls
- BUGANDA
- Mutesa's
- Nyanza
- L. Kivu
- R. Congo
- RWANDA
- KARAGWE
- MASAI LAND
- KIKUYU
- Kilimanjaro △
- Mombasa
- Nyangwe
- MANYEMA
- Ujiji
- UNYAMWEZI
- Urambo
- Unyanyembe
- Pemba I.
- Mtowa
- ULUBA
- L. Tanganyika
- UGOGO
- Pangani
- Zanzibar
- R. Lualaba
- R. Rufiji
- Bagamoyo
- L. Mweru
- INDIAN OCEAN
- L. Mwera
- Kazembe
- LUBEMBA
- Karonga
- Kilwa
- L. Malawi
- R. Rovuma
- Kota Kota

Legend:
- Mirambo's sphere of influence c.1884
- Tippu's sphere of influence c.1884
- --- Arab trade route

Scale: 0 100 200 300 Miles

Arab trade routes about 1840–1884

14 Arab traders move inland

We have seen that Arabs found their way into the interior of Africa between 1840 and 1860. This happened firstly because of the growth of world trade and secondly because of the policy of Sayyid Said. These Arabs were few in number, in a very big country. But they were powerful because their followers carried guns, and because the tribes needed the goods which the Arabs brought to sell.

We have also seen that when the Arab traders went a great distance inland, they were too far from the coast to return each year. For this reason they founded trading settlements, and stayed to live. Such settlements were at Kazembe's on the Luapula, at Karonga on Lake Malawi, at Ujiji on Lake Tanganyika, and at Mutesa's in Buganda. The largest settlement was at Unyanyembe in Nyamwezi country.

Trading chiefs

After a time, the Arabs at some of these places made themselves into chiefs, with authority over the clans and villages far around. Then they would control the ivory and the slave trade in that area. They did this because they wanted to grow wealthy, not because they were interested in the people of the country. They planned that, when they were old, they would retire to the comfort of the coastal town. There they would be able to buy a big house, and settle down with many servants.

At least one African chief followed the example of the Arabs and built up trading empires based on the sale of ivory and slaves.

The people in the villages obeyed the trading chiefs because they were not strong enough to resist, and because they wanted protection from the slave-raiding tribes that began to trouble the country.

As the slave trade grew, there was more war and fighting. In Malawi and Tanganyika, the Ngoni invasion had broken up many small tribes. The Ngoni themselves had split up into parts. Groups of warriors now wandered about, attacking villages. They were called *ruga ruga*. They served any master who would pay them well. They attacked villages, plundered them, and sold slaves to the Arabs.

In Malawi the Yao raided the smaller tribes for slaves. In

(left)
Tippu Tip
(right)
*An early photograph of
ivory carriers*

north-eastern Zambia the Bemba did the same. The Yao and the Bemba sold the slaves to the Arabs.

Because of all this trouble, the smaller tribes preferred to live under a trading chief, even if he was an Arab. They might not like the Arab, but at least he would protect them from the *ruga ruga*. Let us look at the two greatest of these trader chiefs.

Tippu

Tippu Tip was an Arab who made an empire in the Congo highlands west of Lake Tanganyika. His real name was Muhammad bin Hamid. He was born in Zanzibar, and grew up to be a trader on the Unyanyembe route.

When Tippu came to Unyanyembe in 1850, he saw that to obtain more ivory it was necessary to rule the tribes. In this way he could be sure that ivory from every elephant killed would be brought to him and to no one else. There were already several Arabs in Unyanyembe, so Tippu crossed Lake Tanganyika and made an empire in the Congo highlands. Here, great herds of elephant roamed the country.

The people of Uluba lived simpler lives than the tribes to the east of Lake Tanganyika, and Tippu easily subdued them. He fought the Bemba south of the lake, and defeated them as well. Then he went north, down the Congo as far as the Stanley Falls, and said that these lands were to be kept for the trade of the Sultan of Zanzibar.

Tippu ruled all this country as overlord from 1860 to 1884. Twice he came back to Zanzibar with huge expeditions carrying ivory. One expedition carried about two thousand tusks.

In 1885 the Europeans meeting in Berlin said that the Congo basin should be controlled by King Leopold of the Belgians. The Arabs felt that they could not fight the Europeans, so Tippu went back to Zanzibar.

Mirambo

While this was happening west of Lake Tanganyika, another trading empire was built up east of the lake. In Unyamwezi, the Arabs had their settlement at Unyanyembe. At first, the Nyamwezi people were friendly to the Arabs. Then, after 1850, trade increased. The Nyamwezi decided that they should share in the gain from this trade, and Chief Manua Sera tried to make the Arabs pay tax. The Arabs refused, and there was fighting between them.

In 1865 Mirambo became a Nyamwezi chief. He was not

The Stanley Falls and rapids on the River Congo

An illustration of 1861 showing a slave chain-gang in Central Africa

the chief of the whole Nyamwezi people, but he was a strong character and became the most powerful chief in the country. He made his capital at Urambo, about fifty miles from Unyanyembe.

Trade began to go to Urambo instead of Unyanyembe, and Mirambo became stronger than the Arabs. He built forts called *bomas*, with great mud walls, in different parts of his country. *Ruga ruga* came to fight for him, and he extended his rule to Ujiji on Lake Tanganyika, and as far as Ugogo in the east.

Mirambo's empire lasted until his death in 1883. Two years later, German ships came to Zanzibar, and forced the Sultan to agree that the trade of the interior as far as Lake Tanganyika should belong to Germany.

Sultan Barghash

Let us see what was happening on the coast in the time of Tippu and Mirambo.

The great Sayyid Said had died in 1865. He was succeeded, first by Sultan Majid, and then in 1870 by Sultan Barghash. Barghash was not as ambitious as Sayyid Said, but he was a good and wise ruler.

Barghash became a friend of the British consul at Zanzibar, Sir John Kirk. Kirk said that the slave trade was bad and ought to be stopped. He said that if it were not stopped, the British Government would send ships to prevent Zanzibar from trading with anyone. Barghash agreed to do as Kirk asked. He made laws stopping the shipment of slaves from Zanzibar, and closed the Zanzibar slave market.

This made it more difficult for traders from inland to sell their slaves, so the slave trade gradually grew less. At the same time the ivory trade began to decrease because so many elephants had been destroyed.

Finally in 1885, as we have seen, the German Government forced the Sultan to give them the trade of the interior. After this, the Arabs made one more attempt to have a trading empire. It did not last for long.

Mlozi

Because of German activity, some of the Arabs decided to move south, and open up a new slave and ivory trade between Lake

Arab slave convoy: an artist's impression

Malawi and the Luapula. Slaves and ivory from here were brought to Kilwa, and sent away in ships.

The most important 'Arab' taking part in this trade was Mlozi. He was not really Arab, but Swahili. Mlozi made his settlement near Karonga in Lungonde, at the north end of Lake Malawi. Many slaves were sent to Kilwa from Ngonde, Henga, Tumbuka, Mambwe and Tabwa country. Some were even sent from Kazembe's lands on the Luapula.

In 1887 the missionaries at the north end of Lake Malawi tried to drive out Mlozi, but they were not strong enough. They tried to teach the people to grow crops so that they could buy their cloth from the Europeans instead of from the Arabs. But this takes a long time, and there was too much fighting to allow the people to settle down and learn.

In 1891, however, Nyasaland became part of a British Protectorate, and at last in 1895 the British Commissioner, Harry Johnston, arrived with troops. He defeated Mlozi and put him to death. A few Arabs escaped to the Luapula, but soon they too submitted to the British.

A British warship destroying a slave dhow on the east coast of Africa: a mid-19th century drawing

The Arabs in Buganda

In the north, the people of the lake region were too strong for the Arabs to make an empire. Arab traders lived at the Kabaka's capital, but they were guests and paid respect to the Ganda king.

Because the Arabs were in their country, the Ganda people became wealthy and powerful. They took all the Arab trade, and prevented it from going to the kingdoms of Butoro and Bunyoro. They were able to do this because, after passing through Karagwe, Buganda is the first country which traders come to from Unyanyembe.

The Arab trader Muley bin Salim taught the religion of Islam to the Ganda, and by 1875 Kabaka Mutesa was a Moslem. He took on some of the Moslem customs, copied some of the manners of the Sultan of whom he had heard, and lived in greater state than before.

Changes brought by the Arabs inland

We have seen how the Arabs lived and traded in the interior from 1840 to 1890. This is quite a short time, but important changes in the life of the people happened as a result.

First, the slave trade increased greatly. By 1860, twenty thousand slaves a year were sold in the Zanzibar market. There were also smaller markets in the other towns.

Second, the slave trading led to more wars between tribes. Tippu and Mirambo kept peace and order in the centre of their countries. But outside these countries, tribes fought one another in order to take prisoners captive, and sell them to the Arabs for cloth and guns. Many villages were burned and people killed in this way.

Third, many more guns came into the country. Some tribes gave up fighting with spears, and used guns instead. They also used guns for hunting. Elephant and other game began to disappear in parts of the country.

Lastly, more cloth and other goods came into the interior. The custom of making bark cloth began to die out, and so did other customs and crafts which villagers had pursued in more peaceful days.

Arab influence declines

As we have seen, the Arabs were driven out when the Europeans came to control this part of Africa.

European interest in Africa had been growing since the end of the eighteenth century. This interest had been awakened by the journeys of James Bruce in Ethiopia (1768–71) and of Mungo Park along the Niger (1796 and 1805). With the coming of the factory system and new methods of transport, people in Europe saw the possibilities of developing other continents and of bringing Christianity and education to their peoples. Africa, a huge continent, lay close to them, but they knew little about it. By 1860, however, brave travellers had made their way into the interior: René Caillé, Richard Lander and Heinrich Barth across the Sahara to the Niger; Richard Burton and John Speke from the east coast to the source of the Nile; David Livingstone from the Atlantic to the Indian Ocean by way of the Zambezi.

The Peace Museum, built on the site of the old Zanzibar slave market

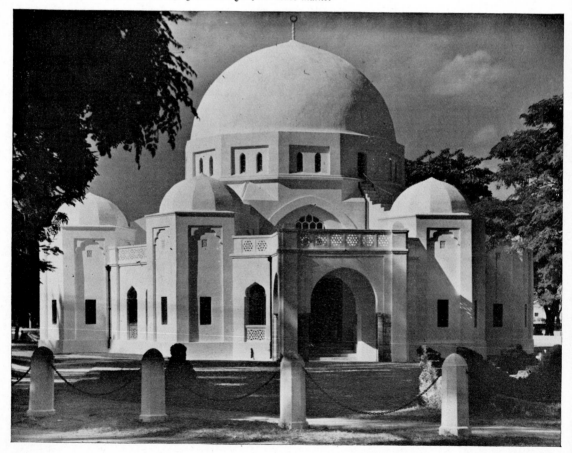

Using quinine and other medicines to protect themselves from tropical disease, other travellers and traders followed.

The early travellers and traders in East Africa, and the missionaries who came with them, saw that the slave trade was cruel and wrong. They remembered how the similar trade to the West Indies had recently been stopped, and asked their governments to end the fighting and slaving in East Africa as well.

The European governments, especially that of Great Britain, were anxious to end the slave trade, but were unwilling to spend the necessary money. However, they saw that proper trade might help to pay for the cost of administration. Above all, business men wanted to be able to import minerals and raw materials, and to be able to sell goods made in their factories to the people of Africa as well as of other continents.

For these reasons, when European control of East and Central Africa began after 1880, slave trading and Arab influence in the interior quickly disappeared. Of course, although the slave markets were closed, Arab and Swahili traders continued living in the east coast towns, where they are important even to this day.

15 West Africa and the Fulani

In the last six chapters we have been reading about developments in East Africa, both on the coast and inland, roughly during the four centuries from 1450 to 1850.

We shall now cross the continent again to West Africa to see what was happening there. First, look back to Chapters 4 and 8. These chapters will remind you of two important events that had affected West Africa in the fifteenth and sixteenth centuries. The first was the coming of European traders to the coast. The growth of the slave trade and of foreign influence helped to change the balance of power among the coastal kingdoms. It also slowed their development. The second event was the Moroccan conquest of Songhai after the battle of Tondibi in 1591. This destroyed the civilization of the Niger empires, and broke up western Sudan into small kingdoms.

Thus by the eighteenth century West Africa consisted of many separate states, often trading, but sometimes warring, with one another. The great systems of Mali and Songhai had long disappeared. Even the powerful city states of Oyo and Benin had become corrupt and lost their influence. In the Niger cities, learning and Moslem worship had declined.

Revival begins

At the end of the eighteenth century, however, new efforts began to create new states and to revive religion and learning. These efforts were made in the Sudan region, north of the forest belt, in areas where the effects of the slave trade had hardly reached.

Here, on the Upper Niger, were the old city states of Segu, Timbuktu and Djenne. Farther east, the Hausa towns continued to trade between the desert and the south, and often to fight with one another. At this time the strongest among them were first Zamfara and then Gobir. To the east again lay Bornu and the dusty villages of Kanem.

All these states had long been Moslem in name, but good Moslem teachers had become few. Pilgrimages to Mecca were rare, and rulers had given up strict Moslem laws and made use of pagan custom. A great religion, however, cannot die away easily, for there are always efforts to renew it. This happened in West Africa.

The Fulani

This Moslem revival started among the Fulani of Hausaland. These nomadic cattle-herdsmen were Hamitic or Berber in type, rather than Negro. Their original home was far to the west, around the headwaters of the Senegal River, in the country called Tekrur. Once subjects of the kingdom of Old Ghana, they had for centuries been wandering eastward, leaving settlements all along the Niger. Since 1450 they had become numerous in Hausaland and Bornu. Some lived in the towns, but most of them remained herdsmen in the countryside.

Many Fulani had become Moslem. The country Fulani, however, kept a purer faith than the townsmen who, as we have seen, had increasingly mixed with the Negro inhabitants and turned back to local custom. One particularly strong Moslem group were the Toronkawa, a Fulani tribe with some Arab blood.

Fulani villagers

Usuman dan Fodio

To this Toronkawa branch of the Fulani belonged Usuman dan Fodio, leader of the greatest religious revival in West Africa since the Almoravids. Claiming descent from an early Fulani chief in Senegal, Usuman was born in Gobir in 1754. Well taught by his father and uncles, he became a devout Moslem. When he was only twenty years old he began preaching tours in Hausa towns, where he soon won many followers.

For thirty years Usuman continued teaching and preaching, mainly in Gobir. He published booklets in Arabic and poems in the Hausa language. Many people listened to him and read his books.

Naturally Usuman found himself increasingly in trouble with the authorities in Gobir. In 1788 the Sultan of Gobir plotted his death, but Usuman had too many supporters, and instead the Sultan had to grant him freedom to preach whenever he wanted. Ten years later the new Sultan Nafata made another attempt to stop the new movement by forbidding conversions to Islam, and also by banning the wearing of turbans, which was customary among Usuman's followers.

In spite of these efforts, the new movement grew steadily year by year. At last in 1803 Nafata's son, Yunfa, a former pupil of Usuman's who had changed his mind when he became Sultan, decided that his position would not be secure as long as Usuman lived. He planned to kidnap Usuman at Degel and have him killed.

The *jihad* begins

Usuman was warned of the plot, and on 21 February 1804, he escaped to Gudu just in time. His followers called this escape the *Hijra*, thus comparing it with the Prophet Mohammed's escape from Mecca in 622.

Usuman, now known as the Shehu, decided that the time had come to wage a holy war, or *jihad*, against the unbelievers of Gobir. His message was simple. In Hausaland there were many pagans. Furthermore, many who were Moslems in name had given up the true faith. True Moslems should withdraw from the society of these unbelievers and pretenders and join the *jihad* against them. Gobir especially, he argued, was an infidel state because its ruler had shown himself to be no longer a Moslem and because of the superstitious practices followed there.

Within a few months the Shehu had raised a large force

from followers who flocked to join him. In June 1804 his army defeated the Sultan of Gobir at the battle of Tabkin Kwotto.

As a result of this victory, many new supporters, mostly Fulani, joined the Shehu's army. They looked far beyond Gobir. The *jihad* was turning from a local religious campaign into a war of conquest. Usuman himself did not take much part in the fighting; a great scholar rather than a soldier, he wrote pamphlets and booklets for the guidance of his followers. His brother, Abdullah, and his son, Mohammed Bello, took command of the armies. After four years of fighting they captured Gobir and killed the Sultan in October 1808.

By this time most of Hausaland was controlled by the Shehu. In the following year, 1809, he made a new capital for his growing empire at Sokoto.

The *jihad* in Bornu

To the east of Hausaland lay Bornu. Here some of the Shehu's enemies had taken refuge. The Shehu therefore made war on Bornu and conquered it. The last of the Sefawa kings was turned off his throne, bringing the thousand-year-old dynasty to an end.

However, east of Bornu again lay the old kingdom of Kanem, whose ruler, El Kanemi, was a learned man and a devout Moslem. El Kanemi denied that the people of Bornu were pagans, or that they had become pagans by harbouring the enemies of Usuman. They were true believers, and the Shehu had been quite wrong to make war on them.

El Kanemi therefore raised an army himself, and finally drove Mohammed Bello out of Bornu in 1810. Consequently Bornu and Kanem remained outside the Fulani Empire.

The Fulani Empire

Most of Hausaland, however, was now ruled by the Fulani followers of the Shehu. Usuman himself died in 1817, but the administration was carried on by Mohammed Bello, who became Sultan of Sokoto and controlled the northern part from Zamfara to Kano, and by Abdullah, whose capital was at Gwandu and who looked after the southern area around Nupe and Ilorin.

While the empire was being built up, each expedition commander had been given a flag of authority by the Shehu. These commanders were therefore known as flag-bearers. As each province was conquered, the flag-bearer was appointed as emir

The Fulani Empire
about 1830

to run the civil administration. All but one of these emirs were Fulani.

The emirs ruled according to principles laid down by the Shehu, who himself had made a careful study of Moslem law. These principles covered such things as the working of the law courts, the collection of taxes, the control of the treasury and the administration of markets.

As time went on, the authority of the Sultans of Sokoto and Gwandu grew less, until each Fulani emirate became virtually independent, though continuing to pay tribute. The Fulani leaders intermarried with the local Hausa populations of the towns. None the less the Fulani Empire continued to exist until the British gained control of Hausaland at the end of the century. Its law and administration have continued to influence the government of Northern Nigeria down to the present day.

The Five Rules of Government

... and I say—and help is with God—the foundations of government are five things: the first is that authority shall not be given to one who seeks it. The second is the necessity for consultation. The third is the abandoning of harshness. The fourth is justice. The fifth is good works.

And as for its ministers, they are four. The first is a trustworthy wazir to wake the ruler if he sleeps, to make him see if he is blind, and to remind him if he forgets; and the greatest misfortune for the government and the subjects is that they should be denied honest wazirs. And among the conditions pertaining to the wazir is that he should be steadfast in compassion to the people, and merciful towards them. The second of the ministers of government is a judge whom the blame of a blamer cannot overtake concerning the affairs of God. The third is a chief of police who shall obtain justice for the weak from the strong. The fourth is a tax-collector who shall discharge his duties and not oppress the subjects.

Usuman dan Fodio

16 Influences on Africa's history

We have now read about the story of Africa and its peoples as far as about 1850. Many books recount the events that happened after that, as the result of trading and colonizing competition among the European powers. The aim of this short chapter is not to go further forward with the story, but to look back and to sum up the situation at that time.

To begin with, let us consider what have been the greatest forces influencing Africa's development during the past two thousand years. We can pick out seven main ones.

The foundations

First, there is the land itself. A massive continent, Africa has two notable characteristics. One is its isolation. Although close to, and in fact linked with, Europe and Asia, its interior is difficult to approach, partly because of the desert barrier in the north and partly because its rivers are not navigable very far. The second characteristic is that Africa lies across the equator. This gives much of it a decidedly tropical climate. The effects of this climate on human development have been described in this book. It has also meant that the same conditions are to be found in the north and south of the continent. The peoples of Africa have been able to move from one part to another and find familiar grasslands, forests, deserts or mountains. This has perhaps encouraged the migrations that are a feature of Africa's history.

This brings us to the second big influence on the history of Africa: its peoples. We have seen that these are a blend of aboriginal types with Negroes and Hamites, and with some Semitic and European elements as well. The largest groups are the Negroes and their cousins, the Bantu-speaking peoples, and to these we usually apply the word 'African': they are the chief inhabitants of tropical Africa. Truly, however, all inhabitants of the continent could be called African. They are varied and vigorous peoples, with great cultures of their own, all of whom have played a part in the important story of human development that belongs to the African continent.

Thirdly, there is the influence of Ancient Egypt. One of the earliest and greatest civilizations in the world, the Egyptian civilization lasted for three thousand years. That is twice as long as European civilization, which has grown out of the ruins of the Roman Empire. It happened on the African continent, and its peoples were Africans of one kind or another. Though separated from tropical Africa by the desert belt, the influence of Egyptian belief and custom, passing through Meroe, has been felt in different ways all through the continent ever since. Some of these ways have been described in this book.

Religion

The fourth great influence has been the religion of Islam. This influence has of course been greatest in North Africa and in the Western Sudan from the Upper Nile to the Upper Niger. Here it has formed the faith of millions of people, and made possible study and learning. Sometimes it has caused religious wars. It has also helped to create large states like the Songhai Empire, in which people have been able to live together in peace and order. The east coast of Africa also has been marked by the civilizing influence of Islam; but here the Arab and Persian settlers usually put trade before religion. Islam did not spread inland until about a hundred years ago, when Christian missionaries were also at work.

This fifth great influence, Christianity, did not affect most of Africa until after the period covered by this book. Christianity in North Africa declined after the Romans left, except in Egypt, and finally disappeared when the Moslems came. The Christian church of Aksum, later Abyssinia, remained cut off in the Ethiopian highlands until recent times. Portuguese attempts to convert Africans after 1500 in West Africa, Angola and Mashonaland met with little success and were spoilt by trading ambitions, and especially by the slave trade. Christianity did not really begin to come to most of Africa until the European explorers showed the way for the missionaries in the nineteenth century. At that time medical discoveries were also making it possible for Europeans to live in a tropical climate.

Two of the great things the Christian church then did were first to insist on the slave trade being stopped, and second to help the African peoples through the difficult seventy years of colonial rule, especially with education. However, those achievements lie outside the scope of this book, which has told the story of Africa before the partition began.

The sixth influence has been foreign trade. In spite of its isolation for reasons which we have seen, there has been some trade between Africa and the rest of the world for thousands of years. It has always been the possibilities of trade which have drawn foreign peoples into Africa. Even across the Sahara this trade has taken place, helping to create the wealth which built the empires of the Niger. The rest of Africa, of course, could only be reached by using ships. The Indian Ocean trade along the east coast, as we have seen, was a very old one. It was not till the Europeans learnt to sail far out on the oceans after 1400 that the great trading peoples of Portugal, Holland, France and England began to reach Africa. Their trade grew, at first slowly, and then after 1850 very quickly. Slaves were only a part of this trade though, for a time, a large part. By 1850 slave trading by European countries had been stopped, and had been replaced entirely by the exchange of manufactured goods for raw materials.

None the less it is a fact of Africa's history that trade, which should have been a useful and civilizing influence, often did more harm than good at the beginning. Too often it promoted war or disturbance, and helped to break up growing African states like Oyo and Benin in the west, Mbanza Kongo in the centre, and Monomotapa's empire in the south-east. More recently the harm done to the Congo region by the oil and rubber trade in the time of the Congo Free State is well known. Perhaps this was because much early trade was not real trade, but involved the use of force and deception.

One of the great difficulties about trade in Africa has of course always been the absence of proper transport and communications. Only since they have been provided in this century has Africa really begun to benefit from trade.

This brings us to the seventh and final influence, which has been the period of colonial rule. This began in most parts of Africa after 1875, and ended in most parts after 1960. You can read about this in other books. The many effects of this period are obvious to anyone living in Africa, from political boundaries and ways of government and official languages to roads and mines and railways. Here we shall just say three things about it.

First, it was probably inevitable, because European countries which experienced the industrial revolution were growing rich and powerful so quickly compared with other parts of the world.

Some good as well as bad effects resulted. These bad effects probably ought to have been prevented, but the colonial period as a whole was bound to come.

Second, it is unlikely that Africa could have caught up with the modern world in any other way. Even now Africa is still catching up. The old, really African cultures are still growing together with modern ways of life. This growing together will continue for a long time. It is a good process. It is only from the mixing together of different influences that new good ideas can come. This will happen in Africa.

In the last century it was not so easy to see this. To conclude, we shall turn back once more to look at the condition of Africa a hundred years ago.

Africa a hundred years ago

When foreign travellers made their way into the continent during the last century, they found a great deal of disorder. If you look through the time charts in this book, you will see that this was so, and perhaps why it was so. In the western Sudan the Negro states, as a result of the Fulani *jihads*, were only just beginning to recover from the effects of the Moroccan invasion three hundred years before. In the forest belt of the west coast, wars caused by slave trading continued to make settled life difficult, while Oyo and Benin had grown feeble and corrupt. The same conditions affected the Congo region. In East Africa the appearance of Arab traders inland brought slave trading and war, and the spread of guns and powder. All south-east Africa was also disturbed by the effects of the *mfecane* wars in Natal. These had been partly caused by the conflict between the southern Bantu and the Boers. They resulted in warrior tribes like Ndebele and Ngoni migrating north and bringing war to the lands north of the Limpopo.

All this encouraged foreign visitors to describe Africa as a barbaric land of war and disorder. Many books gave this description. However, we can see that it was not altogether true, because not all Africa was disturbed like this. More important, Africa's past was far from being always a period of disorder. To a large extent it was foreign invasion and the wrong kinds of foreign trade during the previous three centuries which had helped to make these conditions prevail.

Anyone who reads thoughtfully about Africa's past will see that history is not one long story of upward progress. It is a story of stops and starts, of going forward and then backward before going forward again. One thing which is certain is that Africa today is at the beginning of the greatest stride forward in all her history so far.

North African Time Chart

Date	West Africa	North Africa	Ethiopia
B.C. 500 400	Early Berber trade across the Sahara.	Phoenicians settling on North African coast.	More Hamites from Arabia settling in Ethiopia.
300 200	Iron Age reaches Nok community on Jos Plateau.	Rise of Carthage begins. Conquest of Carthage by Rome in the Punic Wars. Roman rule in N. Africa begins.	
100 **A.D.**		Roman rule completed by conquest of Egypt.	Growth of Aksum with port at Adulis as centre of trade between Upper Nile and Red Sea.
100	Small Mandingo chiefdoms on the Upper Niger River.		
200 300		Greatest extent of Roman Empire.	Aksum now capital of great kingdom. King Ezana destroys Meroe. First obelisks set up. Christianity accepted in Aksum.
400 500 600	Berber kings begin to rule in Ghana.	End of Roman Empire in west. Vandals overrun N. Africa. Destruction of towns like Leptis. Berber tribes alone survive. Camel reaching Sahara.	Great age of Aksum.
		THE *HIJRA* 622	
700	Za kings begin to rule in Gao.	Arabs conquer Egypt. Arabs conquer the Mahgrib, cross to Spain. Abbasids overthrow Umayyads, found new capital at Baghdad.	Aksum cut off by Mohammedan conquests. 'Dark Age' of Aksum begins.
800 900	Soninke (Negro) kings establish rule in Ghana. Visit of El Fazari.	Beginning of Fatimid Empire in N. Africa. Cairo founded.	Appeal from King of Aksum to King of Nubia goes unanswered.
1000 1100 1200	Kingdom of Ghana at greatest extent. Almoravid conquest. Islam begins in Ghana. Collapse of Almoravid rule. Sundiata founds Empire of Mali.	Beginning of Almoravid Empire. Ghana conquered. Almohads replace Almoravids in the Mahgrib. Mahgrib breaks up into separate states.	Zagwe line of kings set up. Rock-hewn churches built. Centre of kingdom moves south to Amhara. Last Zagwe king overthrown. Solomonic line restored.
1300	Growth of Islam along Niger. Musa's *hadj* to Mecca. Mali Empire at greatest extent.		
1400 1500	Sonni Ali founds Empire of Songhai. Askia I conquers Mali (1590). Greatest extent of Songhai-Moroccan wars. End of Songhai Empire.		Conquests of King Zara Yakob. New Moslem invasion. Appeal to Portuguese for help. Moslems driven from Abyssinia. Isolation of Abyssinia continues.
1600 1700		Moroccans overthrow Songhai at Tondibi (1591). Moroccans withdraw to north of desert.	
1800	Fulani Empire begins.		

Questions and exercises

These questions are included for general guidance. Teachers will of course have other exercises and questions of their own. In particular, pupils should be encouraged to illustrate their notebooks with maps and drawings taken from the text.

Chapter 1
1 Explain why Al Mahgrib became separated from the rest of the Arab Empire.
2 Write a paragraph about Ibn Yasin and why he was important.
3 What influence did the Almoravids have on West Africa?

Chapter 2
1 Explain the importance of gold, slaves and salt to the trade of Ghana.
2 What developments took place in Ghana under the Soninke kings?
3 What were the effects of the Almoravid conquest upon Ghana?

Chapter 3
1 Write a short life of Sundiata.
2 Imagine that you accompanied Mansa Musa on his pilgrimage to Mecca. Describe your experiences.
3 Write down four things reported by Ibn Batuta about the Empire of Mali.

Chapter 4
1 Who were (*a*) the Songhai and (*b*) the Za Kings?
2 Compare the character and achievements of Sonni Ali and Askia the Great.
3 Explain the importance of the battle of Tondibi.

Chapter 5
1 Explain how Bornu became an important kingdom in 1500.
2 Do you think that the legend of Abuyazidu is a satisfactory account of the beginning of the Hausa Bokwoi? Give reasons.
3 How did the Hausa manage to keep their independence?

Chapter 6
1 Imagine that you are a brass craftsman in Ife about 1300. Describe your work and trade.
2 Why did the Alafin of Oyo become such a powerful ruler?
3 Explain why the Yoruba Empire finally broke up in the eighteenth century.

Chapter 7	1 What was the influence of the Portuguese on the kingdom of the Kongo?
	2 Describe the achievements of Shyama Ngoongo among the Kuba.
	3 Three peoples are described in this chapter—the Kongo, the Kuba and the Luba. Write down two things which interest you about each.

Chapter 8	1 Describe the part played by Henry the Navigator in the Portuguese exploration of West Africa.
	2 Why did the European traders fight against one another more than against the African inhabitants of the west coast?
	3 Why did the Africans not only fail to stop the slave trade, but even take part in it themselves?

Chapter 9	1 Why did the Portuguese first come to East Africa, and why did they seize the Arab towns?
	2 What difficulties did the Portuguese meet with in Mashonaland in the sixteenth and seventeenth centuries?
	3 Why did the Portuguese finally give up most of the East African towns?

Chapter 10	1 Who were the Chwezi? What benefits did they bring to the lake region? What happened to them after the Lwo invasion? Draw a plan of the Bigo earthworks.
	2 Who were the Lwo? Why did they invade the lake region? Make a list of the kingdoms set up by the Lwo.
	3 Who were the Nilo-Hamites? Write a paragraph about their character and beliefs. Why did they think they had a right to other people's cattle? Find out where they live today.
	4 Explain why the Ganda became a powerful tribe.
	5 Why did the Kikuyu not learn to have chiefs until recent times?

Chapter 11	1 Why are some of the Malawi called Mang'anja, while others have different names?
	2 Describe the part played by Chitimukulu I in the history of the Bemba tribe.
	3 What is meant by the 'Lunda dispersal'?

Chapter 12	1 Explain the reasons for the *mfecane* wars.
	2 Describe the effects of the Ngoni migration on countries north of the Zambezi.
	3 How did the Ndebele come to live north of the Limpopo River?

Chapter 12   1 Explain the reasons for the *mfecane* wars.
              2 Describe the effects of the Ngoni migration on countries north of the Zambezi.
              3 How did the Ndebele come to live north of the Limpopo River?

Chapter 13   1 Explain why the Arabs started slave trading in the interior of East Africa after 1800.
              2 Draw a map of Arab trade routes into the interior. Through what African tribes did they pass?

Chapter 14   1 Who were the *ruga ruga*? (See also Chapter 12.) How did they affect developments in East Africa?
              2 Describe the part played by either Tippu or Mirambo in the development of East African trade.
              3 What were the effects of Arab trade in the East African interior?

Chapter 15   1 Who were the Fulani?
              2 Write an account of the life of Usuman dan Fodio in three paragraphs.
              3 What was the importance of the Fulani Empire for that part of West Africa?

Chapter 16   1 Make a list of the seven main influences on the history of Africa. Can you think of any others?
              2 Why did many foreign travellers look upon Africa as a land of barbarism and disorder a hundred years ago?
              3 What do you think were the three most important effects on Africa of the period of colonial rule (not described in this book)?
              4 If you were writing a history of Africa a hundred years from now, what topics would you include for a chapter on the 1960's?

Index

IJA